THE 2001 MATHERS LECTURE, THE 2001 ROSEN LECTURE, AND OTHER QUEEN'S UNIVERSITY ESSAYS IN THE STUDY OF JUDAISM

THE 2001 MATHERS LECTURE, THE 2001 ROSEN LECTURE, AND OTHER QUEEN'S UNIVERSITY ESSAYS IN THE STUDY OF JUDAISM

Edited by Jacob Neusner

With papers by Donald H. Akenson, Herbert Basser, Reena Basser, and Jacob Neusner

Academic Studies in the History of Judaism
Global Publications, Binghamton University
Binghamton, New York
2001

Cover artwork entitled "Huppah" by Suzanne R. Neusner.

Library of Congress Cataloging-in-Publication Data:

The 2001 Mathers lecture, the 2001 Rosen lecture, and other Queen's University essays in the study of Judaism / edited by Jacob Neusner ; With papers by Donald H. Akenson ... [et al.].
p. cm. -- (Academic studies in the history of Judaism)
Includes bibliographical references.
ISBN 1-58684-155-6 (paper back : alk. paper)
1. Judaism--History--Talmudic period, 10-425. 2. Judaism--Relations--Christianity. 3. Christianity and other religions--Judaism. 4. Rabbinical literature--History and criticism. 5. Bible. N.T.--Criticism, interpretation, etc. I. Title: Two thousand and one Mathers lecture. II. Title: 2001 Rosen lecture. III. Neusner, Jacob, 1932- IV. Akenson, Donald H. V. Series.
BM177 .A14 2001
296--dc21

2001005723

Published and Distributed by:
Academic Studies in the History of Judaism
Global Publications, Binghamton University
State University of New York at Binghamton
LNG 99, Binghamton University
Binghamton, New York, USA 13902-6000
Phone: (607) 777-4495 or 777-6104; Fax: (607) 777-6132
E-mail: pmorewed@binghamton.edu
http://ssips.binghamton.edu

ACADEMIC STUDIES IN THE HISTORY OF JUDAISM

Publisher: Global Publications, State University of New York at Binghamton
Address: LNG 99, SUNY-Binghamton, Binghamton, New York 13902-6000

Table of Contents

PREFACE

I

Universities not only sustain scholarship, creating new knowledge and testing the old, but also shape culture. This they do by persuading scholars to address a broad audience with the results of rigorous learning. Lectures for a wide public form a principal means by which university professors shape the intellectual life. They address issues of broad concern, and when they do so, they clarify and deepen public discourse upon them.

But university scholars not only contribute to the public interest by sharing their knowledge, they also gain from serving as public intellectuals. The vocation to speak beyond the limits of specialization imposes its own discipline and presents its own intellectual challenge. Specifically, the academic scholars are challenged to think through the details of their subject-matter in quest of the main point, what matters — makes a difference — to the world at large. And that process of retrospection and introspection provides perspective even on the most arcane, recondite, and technical aspects of their learning and research.

A single example serves to show how much the world gains when the scholar addresses a wide audience out of his special knowledge. It also shows how much scholarship gains by shaping its results for a realm of intellect beyond the narrow limits of specialization. When Gershom G. Scholem presented the Stroock Lectures of the then Jewish Institute of Religion in New York City that became *Major Trends in Jewish Mysticism*, published in 1941, he transformed his subject. He took as his task to show the shape and structure of an entire field of Judaic speculation and praxis, which, until his time, people understood only in bits and pieces. Mysticism in Judaism, until *Major Trends*, accessible only to the initiated, represented a chaotic and pointless chapter in the history of Judaism. Many would gladly have forgotten it, and few accorded the subject the dignity of academic inquiry. Scholem's lectures, widely read and reprinted, changed all that.

Organizing the whole and showing its continuity, structure, and rationality, Scholem explained to a vast audience why Qabbalistic texts were important statements of a complex and profound culture. He made those documents make sense. He provided them with a context and made them coherent. This he did, I maintain, because he was called upon to do so. Whether Scholem would have sat down to tell the story of the whole seen all at once, to show the continuity of persons and movements and ideas and systems of thought, and whether he would have done so with the clarity demanded by a public occasion, no one can know. But the Stroock Lectures form a model of the difference it makes when a scholar takes on the tasks of a public intellectual. And the utilization of such an occasion to prepare lectures not only to be heard but to be read realizes the promise of the setting. Fields that at some point find their Scholem endure for generations; those that do not fade into cultural irrelevance.

Scholem's lectures set the standard, which few can hope to attain in any field, for the public intellectual in preparing a university lecture. When invited to address a University, — an entire community of learning and not only colleagues in my specialty, the study of Judaism, or students in my general discipline, the academic study of Religion, — I have tried to challenge myself with this question: what issue do I identify, within the heritage on which I concentrate, that demands wide public discussion? Of all the things on which I work, the entire repertoire of knowledge that, after forty years of everyday work, I have amassed, what do I select as worth the attention of people who know little about my subject but are willing to learn? Within the theory of the University as principal mediator of culture and intellect to the social order that it serves, these questions define the task. And in that same context, I always publish the lecture, treating the event as an opportunity widely to stimulate to thought about issues of common intelligibility that inhere in my special subject.

II

Part of the task of addressing not specialists, not even a department, its faculty and students, but an entire University is to find issues of broad concern, sources of humanistic interest and general intelligibility. For my Mathers Lecture at Queen's University, I chose the humble task of systematic exposition of an important chapter in Judaism, how the quest for sanctification encompasses the formation of ethical imperatives. That is because Judaism has found itself accused of fostering attitudes of superiority and hypocrisy, the command, "You shall be holy because I the Lord your God am holy" (Lev. 19:2) being treated — so the other side maintains — as occasion to become "holier than thou." To point to the ethical and moral dimensions of the exposition in Leviticus Chapter Nineteen of that opening imperative does not suffice. I determined to spell out, in broad terms, precisely how the Rabbinic sages of the formative age of Judaism, in the Mishnah, Talmuds, and Midrash, set forth the imperatives of sanctification in such a way as to identify the holy with humility and honor, sanctification with service to the other. For that purpose, I have laid my stress upon representative, normative texts and expounded them in a coherent, orderly manner. My purpose is to construct a systematic account of the doctrine of Rabbinic Judaism that links holiness to goodness, in line with Leviticus 19:18, the climactic moment of Judaism's exposition of holiness: "You shall love your neighbor as yourself." On this, everyone knows,

Hillel commented, "That is the entire Torah. All the rest is commentary. Now go, learn."

III

In preserving and circulating the record of the Mathers Lecture, further, I determined to highlight the scholarship of colleagues at Queen's University who specialize in the study of the same time and place in the history of Judaism within the unfolding of Western civilization. As I explain in my formal lecture, I have long regarded Professor Herbert Basser as exemplary scholar and colleague, master of the texts and rigorous exegete thereof. Having joined in the celebration of Professor Donald H. Akenson's work on the formative history of Christianity and Judaism in a single context, I wished also to call attention, on the occasion of my visit to his University, to his remarkable achievement: a generalist able to see matters whole and complete in ways not always perceived by the specialists. Finally, I should not want to have omitted from these pages the work of my counterpart at Queen's University, Professor Reena Basser, specialist in the sources of Judaism in the formative age.

IV

The occasion of the publication of my lecture and Professor Akenson's, as well as the companion scholarly papers of the Professors Basser, allows me the opportunity in print to express thanks, also, to everyone at Queen's University who served as hosts. That includes Professor Jerry Tulchinsky, chairman of Judaic Studies, and the many professors and students of various disciplines and departments who participated in my lecture and in the seminar held on the same occasion. I do not take for granted either their hospitality or their courtesy. Not all universities maintain the high standards of both that characterize Queen's University.

Jacob Neusner
Research Professor of Religion and Theology
Senior Fellow of the Institute of Advanced Theology
Bard College
Annandale-on-Hudson, New York 12504

Neusner@webjogger.net

1

THE ETHICAL IMPERATIVES OF HOLINESS

How in Formative Judaism Theology and Law Come to Realization in Workaday Conduct

The Mathers Lecture
Queen's University

Jacob Neusner
Bard College

To be asked by a major University, one of scholarly ambition in a nation known for the excellence of its universities, to present a lecture in a field in which that University is itself distinguished brings special honor. That is why I am honored to be invited to present The Mathers Lecture at Queen's University. As the entire world of Jewish scholarship knows, Queen's is represented in the galaxy of learning by its superstar in the study of Judaism, Professor Herbert Basser. He is the one whom many in the study of ancient Judaism, myself included, revere as the embodiment of authentic erudition joined to critical, analytical judgment. His books and articles embody a spirit of purity in quest for understanding in the sustaining sources of Judaism. He is the model of authentic, important scholarship in Jewish studies, with his unerring sense for what matters. I am proud to address his University in his field. I am pleased, also, to take note of Professor Reena Basser, his wife, who maintains at Queen's University a high standard of instruction in the classics of Judaism.

I am glad, also, to address the University graced by the esteemed Professor Donald H. Akenson, whose account of the formative age of Judaism and Christianity has done so much to bring *aggiornamento*, up-dating, to that subject. Because of his book, happily recognized with important scholarly honors, the two religions' foundations can never again be studied in isolation from one another. That is no mean academic achievement for a consumer, not a producer — an outsider to the scholarship of the field. But probably could have been accomplished only from the perspective of an outsider — the right outsider.

All of us represented in these pages I concur that academic learning realizes its purpose for humanity when learning yields wisdom, so I have decided to devote this lecture to an exposition of how, in my view, the religion, Judaism, translated the theology of sanctification into practical rules for everyday life. If people should derive, from my exposition of the Rabbinic sages teachings, lessons of wisdom and human worth, I shall have accomplished my purpose.

I
In Judaism, Does "Being Holy" Mean "Holier than Thou"?

Since my purpose is to expound the normative position of Judaism, as portrayed in its canonical sources, about a fundamental conception of holiness, the relationship of the holy to the good, I have to begin by answering a simple question. It is, What, exactly, do I mean by "Judaism," the religious tradition that I expound in this lecture? In this presentation by "Judaism" I mean, the particular religious tradition that sets forth what it holds to be God's revelation at Mount Sinai through Moses to Israel, the holy people. In that connection I cite as the evidence of that religious tradition not ethnic opinion, e.g., "what the Jews believe," but the position of the authoritative canon.

The shank of my lecture is comprised by the texts I have chosen to expound my answer to the question before us, and how I compose those particular texts into a coherent doctrine covering the ethical imperatives of holiness. Which documents supply these texts, and why are they normative?

I cite the Hebrew Scriptures of ancient Israel along with a particular set of documents, the Mishnah, Talmud, and Midrash of late antiquity.[1] Judaism here is defined as the doctrine of law and theology set forth by the Torah. The Torah within the classical system consists of the Written part, Scriptures as we know

[1] How we identify the normative position on a given issue that is taken by Scripture as mediated by the Mishnah, Talmud, and Midrash, with the diverse opinions on any given subject, is simple. I cite as normative for the Torah, written as mediated by the oral, opinion that is not contradicted or that represents the consensus joining sages who differ on detail. I claim that no position cited in this presentation is subject to contradictory rulings or is presented as schismatic or that clearly violates the established consensus of the documents. The one point where I think the system as a whole is subverted comes at the end, and people may judge for themselves my reasons for deemed the systemic reversal as the systemic realization.

them, and the Oral part, finally written down in the Mishnah, Talmud, and Midrash. These canonical works are the media by which the Hebrew Scriptures are presented as a system for holy Israel's social order, that structure of conduct and conviction, behavior and belie, that all together is set forth in the holy books nearly everywhere deemed authoritative by those that practice Judaism.

My question to begin with is, what, in Judaism as just now defined, does "being holy" mean? I deem the question urgent because of a broadly held judgment that holiness stands in opposition to goodness, rite to right. Since, people recognize, Judaism sets forth in its classical statement a regimen intended to sanctify its faithful to form a "kingdom of priests and a holy people," and since that discipline encompasses matters of what goes into the mouth, not only what comes out, Judaism has to explain the way in which sanctification entails ethics, not only ritual. When, in common parlance, we hear the word "holy," we respond by instinct, "holier than thou." Because Israelites are commanded to strive to be holy, meaning, separate and pure, people imagine they are encouraged to feel superior to others. That is because people readily distinguish between the holy and the good. Holiness, then, is associated with arrogance, self-righteousness, and moral *Apartheid.*

But that is not how Judaism, defined by the Rabbinic sages of the formative age, sees matters. In the canonical documents comprised by Scripture as mediated in the Mishnah, Talmuds, and Midrash of ca. 200 through 600 C.E., the sages evince a different instinct altogether. To them, to be holy is to strive to imitate God, to be like God. And in their reading of the Torah, God is just and merciful, so that is how, in order to sanctify themselves, Israelites are supposed to be. In their definitive statement of Judaism, it is difficult to distinguish the holy from the just and righteous and good. To be holy *is* to be like God, who is the realization of justice and mercy.

The philosophical question, is it good because God wants it, or does God want it because it is good? with its distinction what is good and what God wants, in that context does not register. It was Abraham who raised the question when, pleading mercy for Sodom and Gomorrah, he asked, "Shall not the Judge of all the earth deal justly?" (Gen. 18:25) — and it was God who settled the question when he responded, "If I find within the city of Sodom fifty innocent persons, I will forgive the whole place for their sake" (Gen. 18:26). What Abraham found unthinkable God could not contemplate: the distinction between the All-Powerful God and the always-just God — and so throughout.

How then are matters set forth so that holiness means goodness? When at Lev. 19:2, God declares, "You shall be holy, for I the Lord your God am holy," the Rabbinic sages respond, in Sifra, their verse by verse reading of the book of Leviticus, with the question: "does God's holiness depend upon our acts of sanctification," and answers that it does not — a different question altogether from the familiar one of medieval and modern ethics, which differentiates between holiness and goodness:

1. A. "And the Lord said to Moses, Say to all the congregation of the people of Israel, You shall be holy, [for I the Lord your God am holy. Every one of you shall revere his mother and his father, and you shall keep my Sabbaths; I am the Lord your God. Do not turn to idols or make for yourselves molten gods; I am the Lord your God]" (Lev. 19:1-4):

B. This teaches that this chapter was stated in the assembly of all Israel.

C. And why was it stated in the assembly of all Israel?

D. It is because most of the principles of the Torah depend upon its contents.

2. A. "You shall be holy":

B. "You shall be separate."

3. A. "You shall be holy, for I the Lord your God am holy":

B. That is to say, "if you sanctify yourselves, I shall credit it to you as though you had sanctified me, and if you do not sanctify yourselves, I shall hold that it is as if you have not sanctified me."

C. Or perhaps the sense is this: "If you sanctify me, then lo, I shall be sanctified, and if not, I shall not be sanctified"?

D. Scripture says, "For I...am holy," meaning, I remain in my state of sanctification, whether or not you sanctify me.

E. Abba Saul says, "The king has a retinue, and what is the task thereof? It is to imitate the king."

Sifra CXCV:I

The normative reading of the commandment of holiness, I contend, leaves no possibility of making the distinction deemed self-evident by those who frame matters as I just did: is it good because God wants it, or does God want it because it is good? Such a distinction simply does not compute. How creatures are to imitate their creator is made explicit in Scripture, for Leviticus 19 immediately introduces, as articulations of sanctification, a systematic articulation of the Ten Commandments, for instance, honor of parents, not making images of God, care for the poor, not stealing, not deceiving, not swearing falsely, fearing God by not insulting the deaf or placing a stumbling block before the blind (Lev. 19:14). The systematic exposition of the concretization of holiness ends with the golden rule, "You shall not take vengeance or bear a grudge against your fellow. You shall love your neighbor as yourself, I am the Lord" (Lev. 19:18). The commandment to love is deemed fundamental by the great religions of the world, among them, Judaism. That is shown by the amplification of the passage in Sifra:

1. A. "You shall not hate your brother in your heart, [but reasoning, you shall reason with your neighbor, lest you bear sin because of him. You shall not take vengeance or bear any grudge against the sons of your own people, but you shall love your neighbor as yourself: I am the Lord]" (Lev. 19:17-18).

4. A. "You shall not take vengeance [or bear any grudge]":
B. To what extent is the force of vengeance?
C. If one says to him, "Lend me your sickle," and the other did not do so.
D. On the next day, the other says to him, "Lend me your spade."
E. The one then replies, "I am not going to lend it to, because you didn't lend me your sickle."
F. In that context, it is said, "You shall not take vengeance."

5. A. "...or bear any grudge":
B. To what extent is the force of a grudge?
C. If one says to him, "Lend me your spade," but he did not do so.
D. The next day the other one says to him, "Lend me your sickle,"
E. and the other replies, "I am not like you, for you didn't lend me your spade [but here, take the sickle]!"
F. In that context, it is said, "or bear any grudge."

6. A. "You shall not take vengeance or bear any grudge against the sons of your own people":
B. "You may take vengeance and bear a grudge against others."

7. A. "...but you shall love your neighbor as yourself: [I am the Lord]":
B. R. Aqiba says, "This is the encompassing principle of the Torah."
C. Ben Azzai says, "'This is the book of the generations of Adam' (Gen. 5:1) is a still more encompassing principle."

Sifra CC:III

Among the great Rabbinic sages, Aqiba is joined by Hillel, who framed matters in negative terms and in Aramaic, "What is hateful to yourself, do not do to your fellow. That is the entire Torah. All the rest is commentary. Now go, study!" (B. Shabbat 30b). Now that we have laid to rest the commonplace dismissal of holiness as opposed to ethics, or rite and right, we have to ask ourselves, what, precisely, does Judaism define as the ethical imperatives of holiness, and how in Judaism do theology and law come to realization in everyday behavior in imitation of God?

II.
The Source of Virtue in Judaism
The Ground of Ethical Conduct in God's Example

For Judaism the virtuous person imitates the virtue of God. So Judaism's account of virtue and ethical conduct begins in the Torah's picture of world order based on God's virtue, not the virtue of humanity. God's traits of justice and equity, love and compassion, form the model for God's creatures. The virtues that Judaism teaches are supposed to characterize the individual and the community. Both are to conduct themselves in God's image, after God's likeness: "Just as I am merciful and long-suffering, so you must be merciful and long-suffering," says the Talmud in its amplification of the commandment to be holy like God.

The doctrine of virtue, which yields ethical teachings for right conduct, finds its context in the scriptural narrative. Humanity, represented by Adam and Eve is created by God "in our image...after our likeness" (Gen. 1:26). Then the matter of virtue finds its context in Adam's and Eve's relationship with God. That relationship was disrupted by Adam's and Eve's disobedience to God's commandment. Then, like Adam and Eve, we too are in God's image, after God's likeness. In their model, we — humanity at large — by our nature both enjoy free will and disobey God's commandments. Virtue then begins in an attitude of voluntary obedience to, and vice in an attitude of rebellion against, God. And ethical conduct is defined by appeal to God's will, expressed in the Torah as interpreted by the Rabbinic sages of Judaism.

Virtue and the consequent practical ethics stand for those traits that bring about reconciliation between Adam and Eve and God, and vice for traits or activities those that disrupt the relationship. So the working-system of the Torah finds its dynamic in the struggle between God's plan for creation — to create a perfect world of justice — and the free will of humanity. All virtuous traits then find their place within that encompassing vision that explains who we are by telling the story of creation culminating in Adam, Eve, and Eden. That is to say, in Judaism "we" are Adam and Eve, fallen from Eden, and, when possessed of the Torah, able to regain Eden. All virtue is defined in that context, and the story that Scripture tells sets forth that context.

III.
Scripture the Source of Virtue.
The Case of Humility over Arrogance

Judaism defines ethical conduct in the model of Scripture's account of the matter. When sages wish to investigate a question, they turn to Scripture, their principal source of facts concerning the record of humanity. There they meet God and in Scripture they amass those established data that supply the answer to any important question. In the Torah they find out that arrogance is a vice and causes sin, while humility is a virtue, and there they learn the reason why: virtue begins in our relationship to God, commencing with that of Adam and Eve: humility and obedience or arrogance and rebellion. Here is how the sages discover the governing principles of virtuous living, a full picture of the matter. What we see is the center of the Judaic doctrine of ethics: the practice of humility over arrogance:

13. A. Whence [in Scripture] do we derive an admonition against the arrogant?

B. Said Raba said Zeiri, "'Listen and give ear, do not be proud' (Jer. 13:15)."

C. R. Nahman bar Isaac said, "From the following: 'Your heart will be lifted up, and you will forget the Lord your God' (Deut. 8:14).

D. "And it is written, 'Beware, lest you forget the Lord your God' (Deut. 8:11)."

15. A. "With him also who is of a contrite and humble spirit" (Is. 57:15).

B. R. Huna and R. Hisda:

C. One said, "I [God] am *with* the contrite."

D. The other said, "I [God] *am* the contrite."

E. Logic favors the view of him who has said, "I [God] am with the contrite," for lo, the Holy One, blessed be he, neglected all mountains and heights and brought his Presence to rest on Mount Sinai,

F. and he did not raise Mount Sinai upward [to himself].

Now the same matter is expressed in general terms, the point being made explicit:

G. R. Joseph said, "A person should always learn from the attitude of his Creator, for lo, the Holy One, blessed be he, neglected all mountains and heights and brought his Presence to rest on Mount Sinai,

H. "and he neglected all valuable trees and brought his Presence to rest in the bush."

18. A. R. Avira expounded, and some say it was R. Eleazar, "Come and take note of the fact that not like the trait of the Holy One, blessed be he, is the trait of flesh and blood.

B. "The trait of flesh and blood is that those who are high take note of those who are high, but the one who is high does not take note of the one who is low.

C. "But the trait of the Holy One, blessed be he, is not that way. He is high, but he takes note of the low,

D. "as it is said, 'For though the Lord is high, yet he takes note of the low' (Ps. 138:6)."

25. A. Said R. Joshua b. Levi, "Come and take note of how great are the humble in the sight of the Holy One, blessed be he.

B. "For when the sanctuary stood, a person would bring a burnt-offering, gaining thereby the reward for bringing a burnt-offering, or a meal-offering, and gaining the reward for a meal offering.

C. "But a person who is genuinely humble does Scripture treat as if he had made offerings of all the sacrifices,

D. "as it is said, 'The sacrifices [plural] of God are a broken spirit' (Ps. 51:19).

E. "And not only so, but his prayer is not rejected, as it is said, 'A broken and contrite heart, O God, you will not despise' (Ps. 51:19)."

F. And R. Joshua b. Levi said, "Whoever properly sets his ways in this world will have the merit of witnessing the salvation of the Holy One, blessed be he,

G. "as it is said, 'To him who orders his way I will show the salvation of God' (Ps. 50:23).

H. "Do not read 'orders' but 'properly sets' [his] way."

Bavli Sotah 1:1-2 V.13ff./5A

Arrogance embodies the bad attitude, and reason leads to the expectation that the arrogant will be cut down to size. If the arrogant person repents, however, then he abandons the bad attitude and adopts the good one, of humility, which is the condition of repentance. God is the model of humility, so too Moses. The resurrection of the dead involves the exaltation of the humble — dust itself. Scripture and parable serve to convey these points, but the system at its core insists upon them.

IV.
Social Foundations of the Ethics of Humility set forth by Judaism

Three important doctrines that define the setting of arrogance within the theological framework of the Torah, that is, Judaism.

[1] God formed creation in accord with a plan, which the Torah reveals. World order can be shown by the facts of nature and society set forth in the Torah's plan to conform to a pattern of reason based upon justice. Those who possess the

Torah — Israel, defined as the people to whom God is made manifest through the Torah — know God. Those who do not — the gentiles, defined as idolators — reject God in favor of idols. What happens to each of the two sectors of humanity, respectively, responds to their relationship with God. Israel in the present age is subordinate to the nations, because God has designated the gentiles as the medium for penalizing Israel's rebellion, meaning through Israel's subordination and exile to provoke Israel to repent. Private life as much as the public order conforms to the principle that God rules justly in a creation of perfection and stasis.

[2] What disrupts the perfection of creation is the sole power capable of standing on its own against God's power, and that is humanity's will. What humanity controls and God cannot coerce is humanity's capacity to form intention and therefore choose either arrogantly to defy, or humbly to love, God. This is where Judaism's definition of virtues makes its appearance. In the context established by the pattern of human creation and conduct, the principal virtue is humility, not arrogance. Because humanity defies God, the sin that results from man's rebellion flaws creation and disrupts world order. The paradigm of the rebellion of Adam in Eden governs, the act of arrogant rebellion leading to exile from Eden thus accounting for the condition of humanity.

[3] But, as in the original transaction of alienation and consequent exile, God retains the power to encourage repentance through punishing man's arrogance. In mercy, moreover, God exercises the power to respond to repentance with forgiveness, that is, a change of attitude evoking a counterpart change. Since, commanding his own will, humanity also has the power to initiate the process of reconciliation with God, through repentance, an act of humility, humanity may restore the perfection of that order that through arrogance he has marred. Here we meet a divine virtue that humanity can replicate: mercy, forgiveness, reconciliation. And yet a third class of virtues, those involved in repentance and atonement, the confession of sin and the determination to do good, will surely follow. But everything begins in the virtue of humility.

God ultimately will restore that perfection that embodied his plan for creation. In the work of restoration death that comes about by reason of sin will die, the dead will be raised and judged for their deeds in this life, and most of them, having been justified, will go on to eternal life in the world to come. In the paradigm of humanity restored to Eden is realized in Israel's return to the Land of Israel. That is the view of the Oral Torah. In that world or age to come, however, that sector of humanity that through the Torah knows God will encompass all of humanity. Idolators will perish, and humanity that comprises Israel at the end will know the one, true God and spend eternity in his light. The dead will rise out of their graves, and the age to come will see humanity restored to Eden.

Now, recorded in this way, the story told by the Torah proves remarkably familiar, with its stress on God's justice (to which his mercy is integral), man's correspondence with God in his possession of the power of will, man's sin and

God's response. It follows that Judaism forms its conception of who we are to begin with out of the story of the creation of man and woman in Eden, and it answers the question, who are we really, by reflecting on the story of humanity's beginning, middle, and ending. All of us, Judaism maintains, are formed in the model of Adam and Eve.

If humble obedience to God's will defines virtue, and arrogant rebellion vice, then the question arises, on what account does humanity act with so much pride? For it is not as though humanity had much in which to take pride or foundation for its arrogant attitude. On the contrary, Aqabiah b. Mehalalel says, if we reflect on whence we come and whither we go, we shall attain humility:

> A. Aqabiah b. Mehalalel says, "Contemplate three things, and you will not come to commit a transgression. Know whence you have come, from a fetid drop; and where you are going, to worms and corruption; and before whom you are going to have to give a full accounting of yourself, before the King of kings of kings, the Holy One, blessed be he"
>
> M. Abot 3:1

> A. Whence he comes: from a place of darkness,
> B. ...where he goes, to a place of darkness and gloom,
> C. what he is going to become, dust and worm and maggot,
> D. and who is his judge, the King of kings of kings, the Holy One, blessed be he.
>
> Abot deRabbi Natan XIX:I.2

The amplification of Aqabiah's saying by the later authority links the definition of humanity to the story of creation, birth, and death. Conscience — not sinning — comes about through consciousness of who we really are. So much for personal virtues and the concrete ethical rules that flow from them. What about social ethics?

V.
What are the Social Virtues God Commands?

The social virtues begin with righteousness, which bears the meaning in Hebrew of charity. To be righteous is to love God. That love is best express through acts of charity (philanthropy), which define righteousness better than any other. The mark of righteousness is to desire God, and the righteous always direct their hearts to God:

> "But the Lord afflicted Pharaoh and his house with great plagues because of Sarai, Abram's wife" (Gen. 12:17):
>
> "The righteous shall flourish like the palm-tree, he shall grow like a cedar in Lebanon" (Ps. 92:13).

> Just as a palm tree and a cedar produce neither crooked curves nor growths, so the righteous do not produce either crooked curves or growths. Just as the shade of the palm tree and cedar is distant from the base of the tree so the giving of the reward that is coming to the righteous seems distant. Just as, in the case of the palm tree and the cedar, the very core of the tree points upward, so in the case of the righteous, their heart is pointed toward the Holy One, blessed be he.
>
> That is in line with the following verse of Scripture: "My eyes are ever toward the Lord, for he will bring forth my feet out of the net" (Ps. 25:15). Just as the palm tree and cedar are subject to desire, so the righteous are subject to desire. And what might it be? What they desire is the Holy One, blessed be he.
>
> Leviticus Rabbah XLI:I.1

Charity and righteousness are called by one and the same word, *sedaqah*, because the act of philanthropy represents righteousness above all else.

Charity and righteous deeds outweigh all other commandments in the Torah. Acts of charity are to be conducted with dignity and respect for the poor. Any one who gives a penny to the poor is blessed with six blessings, and anyone who speaks to him in a comforting manner is blessed with eleven. Any one who gives a penny to the poor is blessed with six blessings: 'Is it not to deal your bread to the hungry and bring the poor to your house...when you see the naked' (Is. 58:7) 'then shall your light break forth... .' And anyone who speaks to him in a comforting manner is blessed with eleven: 'If you draw out your soul to the hungry and satisfy the afflicted soul, then shall your light rise in the darkness and your darkness be as noonday, and the Lord shall guide you continually and satisfy your soul in drought...and they shall build from you the old waste places and you shall raise up the foundations of many generations' (Is. 58:10-12)."

God responds to acts of charity: "Every act of charity and mercy that Israelites do in this world brings about peace and great reconciliation between Israel and their father in heaven: 'Thus says the Lord, do not enter into the house of mourning, nor go to lament, nor bemoan them, for I have taken away my peace from this people...even loving kindness and tender mercies (Jer. 16:4) — loving kindness refers to acts of mercy, and 'tender mercies' to charity" (Bavli Baba Batra 1:5 IV;37-38/10a.).

VI.
The Lowest Vice: Intemperance

Sages admire restraint and temperance, marks of humility, so it stands to reason that loss of restraint and intemperance will signify arrogance. Sages do not treat respectfully the person who takes vows. Vow-takers yield to the undisciplined will, to emotion unguided by rational considerations. But intentionality must (ideally) take form out of both emotion and reflection. Vows explode, the fuel of emotion ignited by the heat of the occasion. "Qonam be any benefit I get from you" hardly forms a rational judgment of a stable relationship; it bespeaks a loss of temper, a response to provocation with provocation. Right at the outset the halakhah gives a powerful signal of its opinion of the whole: suitable folk to begin with do not take vows, only wicked people do. That explains in so many words why, if one says, something is subject to "the vows of suitable folk," he has said nothing. Suitable people — *kesheyrim* — make no vows at all, ever.

A distaste for vowing and disdain for people who make vows then characterize the law. People who take vows are deemed irresponsible; they are adults who have classified themselves as children. They possess the power of intentionality but not the responsibility for its wise use. That is why they are given openings toward the unbinding of their vows; they are forced at the same time to take seriously what they have said. Vows are treated as a testing of Heaven, a trial of Heavenly patience and grace. Sanctification can affect a person or a mess of porridge, and there is a difference. Expletives make that difference; these are not admired. To sages language is holy, it is how God forms a relationship with humanity, the medium of divine communication. Vows constitute a disreputable use of the powerful and the holy. And language is holy because language gives form and effect to intentionality. That is why we do admit intentionality — not foresight but intentionality as to honor — into the repertoire of reasons for nullifying vows, as we note in the law of vows that is set forth at Mishnah-tractate Nedarim:

A. They unloose a vow for a man by reference to his own honor and by reference to the honor of his children.
B. They say to him, "Had you known that the next day they would say about you, 'That's the way of So-and-so, going around divorcing his wives,'
C. "and that about your daughters they'd be saying, 'They're daughters of a divorcée! What did their mother do to get herself divorced' [would you have taken a vow]?"
D. And [if] he then said, "Had I known that things would be that way, I should never have taken such a vow,"
E. lo, this [vow] is not binding.

Mishnah-tractate Nedarim 9:9

The normative law rejects unforeseen events as a routine excuse for nullifying a vow; foresight on its own ("had you known...would you have vowed?") plays a dubious role. But when it comes to the intentionality involving honor of parents or children, that forms a consideration of such overriding power as to nullify the vow.

Our final encounter with the social virtues carries us to the notion that the higher virtue is the one that encompasses lesser ones. And the highest virtue is good will, which encompasses every other social virtue of generosity, foresight, neighborliness, and the rest. The worst vice is not envy, bad neighborliness, defaulting on a loan, but ill-will:

> A. [Rabban Yohanan ben Zakkai] said to [his disciples], "Go and see what is the straight path to which someone should stick."
> B. R. Eliezer says, "A generous spirit."
> C. R. Joshua says, "A good friend."
> D. R. Yosé says, "A good neighbor."
> E. R. Simeon says, "Foresight."
> F. R. Eleazar says, "Good will."
> G. He said to them, "I prefer the opinion of R. Eleazar b. Arakh, because in what he says is included everything you say."
> H. He said to them, "Go out and see what is the bad road, which someone should avoid."
> I. R. Eliezer says, "Envy."
> J. R. Joshua says, "A bad friend."
> K. R. Yosé says, "A bad neighbor."
> L. R. Simeon says, "Defaulting on a loan."
> M. (All the same is a loan owed to a human being and a loan owed to the Omnipresent, blessed be he, as it is said, "The wicked borrows and does not pay back, but the righteous person deals graciously and hands over [what he owes]" [Psalm 37:21].)
> N. R. Eleazar says, "Bad will."
> O. He said to them, "I prefer the opinion of R. Eleazar b. Arakh, because in what he says is included everything you say."
>
> Mishnah-tractate Abot 2:8-9

The reason behind the position is explicit: the comprehensive definition is preferred over the episodic one. Yohanan finds in the attitude of good will the source of all specific virtues, because in his view attitude and intention in the end define the human being: we are what we want to be, the world is what we want to make of it. The entire message of the Torah for the virtuous man and woman is summed up in that conviction, which, furthermore, is embodied in the law of Judaism governing the social order.

VII.
What is Personal Virtue in Attitude and Ethics?

The system of Judaism set forth by the sages forms a tight fabric, so that what sages say in a theological setting comes to expression also in the norms of behavior, guided by law not only by supererogatory will. We see that fact when we take up the matter of hope. That defines one of the highest personal virtues — not to despair — and one of the personal virtues that Israel, a defeated and broken-hearted people, most required for itself. In World War II and afterward, the great teachers of Judaism insisted, "For a Jew it is a sin to despair."

How do the sages of the Talmud make that statement in concrete and practical terms? They resorted to a legal point. When does one lose title to property that has left his domain, e.g., a lost object or a missing beast? The message is, When hope is abandoned, then, but only then, all is lost. This point is made in connection with the law of ownership of property. Ownership of property depends upon one's attitude toward the property. This comes to expression in several ways. If one consecrates the property, God through the Temple becomes the owner. An act of will alienates the rights of ownership. If squatters have taken one's field or house, when does the original owner lose title? It is one relinquishes ownership by reason of despairing of recovering possession of the property, that he also loses the rights of ownership. So one may give up property either as a gift to Heaven or as a surrender to bad fortune. Ownership by itself therefore makes little difference; one's attitude toward one's property, on the one side, and one's disposition of possessions, on the other, govern. One does well, therefore, to hold with open arms; one does better to give up ownership of property to Heaven as an act of donation than relinquish ownership to violence as an act of despair.

In addition to hope, sages identified personal virtues as cleanliness, cultic cleanness, leading to spiritual achievements, holiness, humility, fear of sin, true piety, and onward. These are set forth in a hierarchy, leading from one upward to the next, finally to the day of judgment and eternal life. They did not differentiate the carnal from the spiritual but saw all personal virtue as forming a single coherent whole, from the humble quality of promptness onward up to the resurrection of the dead:

A. In this connection R. Phineas b. Yair would say, "Promptness leads to [hygienic] cleanliness, cleanliness to [cultic] cleanness, cleanness to holiness, holiness to humility, humility to fear of sin, fear of sin to true piety, true piety to the Holy Spirit, the Holy Spirit to the resurrection of the dead, the resurrection of the dead to Elijah the prophet [bringing the Day of Judgment]" [Mishnah-tractate Sotah 9:15].

B. "Promptness leads to [hygienic] cleanliness": "And when he made an end of atoning for the holy place" (Lev. 16:20).

C. "...cleanliness to [cultic] cleanness": "And the priest shall make atonement for her, and she shall be clean" (Lev. 12:8).

D. "...cleanness to holiness": "And he shall purify it and make it holy" (Lev. 16:9).

E. "...holiness to humility": "For thus says the High and Lofty One, who inhabits eternity, whose name is holy, 'I dwell in the high and holy place, with the one who is of a contrite and humble spirit" (Is. 57:15).

F. "...humility to fear of sin": "The reward of humility is the fear of the Lord" (Prov. 22:4).

G. "...fear of sin to true piety": "Then you spoke in a vision to your saints" (Ps. 89:20).

H. "...true piety to the Holy Spirit": "Then you spoke in a vision to your saints" (Ps. 89:20).

I. "...the Holy Spirit to the resurrection of the dead": "And I will put my spirit in you and you shall live" (Ez. 37:14).

J. "...the resurrection of the dead to Elijah the prophet of blessed memory": "Behold I will send you Elijah the prophet" (Mal. 3:23).

Song of Songs Rabbah I:V.3

What we see once more is how the system supplies context to all the details. The virtue of personal cleanliness so far as Judaism teaches it finds its meaning in the ladder that leads to holiness, encounter with the Holy Spirit, and ultimately the resurrection of the dead.

But, as we saw earlier, the right attitude, the appropriate intention — these matter most of all. How does individual virtue encompass matters of attitude and emotion? The Written Torah answers the question decisively. Certainly the right attitude that the individual should cultivate begins in the commandment, "You will love your neighbor as yourself," (Lev. 19:18). Here is how sages amplify that matter:

1. A. "You shall not hate your brother in your heart, [but reasoning, you shall reason with your neighbor, lest you bear sin because of him. You shall not take vengeance or bear any grudge against the sons of your own people, but you shall love your neighbor as yourself: I am the Lord]" (Lev. 19:17-18).

B. Might one suppose that one should not curse him, set him straight, or contradict him?
C. Scripture says, "in your heart."
D. I spoke only concerning hatred that is in the heart.

Sages' first point is to define loving one's neighbor as oneself as loving the neighbor in the heart, not harboring a secret enmity, but expressing openly and honestly one's own grievance. So we bear responsibility for those actions that shape our intentionality and attitude; there are things we can do to improve our attitude toward the other and so to foster a proper intentionality toward him or her, and not bearing a grudge is critical. But that involves expressing what troubles us, not holding things in and secretly conspiring, in our own heart, to get even. So we are required to speak forthrightly to the person against whom we have a grievance:

2. A. And how do we know that if one has rebuked him four or five times, he should still go and rebuke him again?
B. Scripture says, "reasoning, you shall reason with your neighbor."
C. Might one suppose that that is the case even if one rebukes him and his countenance blanches?
D. Scripture says, "lest you bear sin."

That means not taking vengeance or bearing a grudge. As is their way, sages translate their teachings into narratives, which exemplify the point in a clear way:

4. A. "You shall not take vengeance [or bear any grudge]":
B. To what extent is the force of vengeance?
C. If one says to him, "Lend me your sickle," and the other did not do so.
D. On the next day, the other says to him, "Lend me your spade."
E. The one then replies, "I am not going to lend it to, because you didn't lend me your sickle."
F. In that context, it is said, "You shall not take vengeance."

5. A. "...or bear any grudge":
B. To what extent is the force of a grudge?
C. If one says to him, "Lend me your spade," but he did not do so.
D. The next day the other one says to him, "Lend me your sickle,"
E. and the other replies, "I am not like you, for you didn't lend me your spade [but here, take the sickle]!"
F. In that context, it is said, "or bear any grudge."

6. A. "You shall not take vengeance or bear any grudge against the sons of your own people":

B. "You may take vengeance and bear a grudge against others."

7. A. "...but you shall love your neighbor as yourself: [I am the Lord]":

B. R. Aqiba says, "This is the encompassing principle of the Torah."

C. Ben Azzai says, "'This is the book of the generations of Adam' (Gen. 5:1) is a still more encompassing principle."

Sifra CC:III.1-7

And we have already noted, at the end, that the first century authority, Rabbi Aqiba, deems love of neighbor to form the most important principle of the entire Torah.

In addition to love of neighbor, one other personal virtue takes priority, and that is, love of God. But sages also value fear of God, that is to say, reverence. Then they ask, which is the better motive for serving God, fear or love? The one coerces, like it or not; the other appeals to our own will, making God's will into our will, rather than our will into God's will. So sages admire those who serve God out of love, but they identify with those who serve God out of reverence. Here is how they state the matter:

A. On that day did R. Joshua b. Hurqanos expound as follows: "Job served the Holy One, blessed be He, only out of love,

B. "since it is said, 'Though he slay me, yet will I wait for him' (Job. 13:15).

C. "But still the matter is in doubt [as to whether it means], 'I will wait for him,' or, 'I will not wait for him.'

D. "Scripture states, 'Until I die I will not put away mine integrity from me' (Job. 27:5).

E. "This teaches that he did what he did out of love."

F. Said R. Joshua, "Who will remove the dirt from your eyes, Rabban Yohanan b. Zakkai. For you used to expound for your entire life that Job served the Omnipresent only out of awe,

G. "since it is said, 'The man was perfect and upright and one who feared God and avoided evil' (Job. 1:8).

H. "And now has not Joshua, the disciple of your disciple, taught that he did what he did out of love."

Mishnah-tractate Sotah 5:5

Joshua takes the view that Job served God out of love, and Joshua does not share that view, valuing service out of reverence more. He refers to his master, Yohanan b. Zakkai, now deceased, who has not lived to hear the exegesis of which he would have disapproved. Fear or reverence is the greater personal virtue because the one who fears will not rebel, that is, such a one is not going to be arrogant. If we serve God out of love, then our own feelings enter into the transaction; we can deny love. But if we serve God out of fear, then obligation takes over, and humility sets in. But that is not the whole story, as we shall see in a moment, for while Job served out of fear, Abraham did so out of fear, and of them all, he was the only truly beloved one. The upshot is quickly stated: sages found both motives — love and fear — admirable, assigning the one to Job, the other to Abraham. But then, in their context, it is Abraham who forms the ideal.

VIII.
Character, good and bad

Good character is defined in various ways, all of them deriving from the Torah. The basic question of good character is answered by appeal to the commandments that, if one does them, mark a person as Godly. But the Torah contains many commandments. Here is how sages define the truly good character. They affirm that all of the commandments serve to form good character, and disobedience to any of them marks bad character. But they recognize a hierarchy of character-forming obligations, a hierarchy that they find in the Written Torah.

B. R. Simelai expounded, "Six hundred and thirteen commandments were given to Moses, three hundred and sixty-five negative ones, corresponding to the number of the days of the solar year, and two hundred forty-eight positive commandments, corresponding to the parts of man's body."

D. "David came and reduced them to eleven: 'A Psalm of David: Lord, who shall sojourn in thy tabernacle, and who shall dwell in thy holy mountain? (i) He who walks uprightly and (ii) works righteousness and (iii) speaks truth in his heart and (iv) has no slander on his tongue and (v) does no evil to his fellow and (vi) does not take up a reproach against his neighbor, (vii) in whose eyes a vile person is despised but (viii) honors those who fear the Lord. (ix) He swears to his own hurt and changes not. (x) He does not lend on interest. (xi) He does not take a bribe against the innocent' (Psalm 15)."

V. "Isaiah came and reduced them to six: '(i) He who walks righteously and (ii) speaks uprightly, (iii) he who despises the gain of oppressions, (iv) shakes his hand from holding bribes, (v) stops his ear from hearing of blood (vi) and shuts his eyes from looking upon evil, he shall dwell on high' (Isaiah 33:25-26).

FF. "Micah came and reduced them to three: 'It has been told you, man, what is good, and what the Lord demands from you, (i) only to do justly and (ii) to love mercy, and (iii) to walk humbly before God' (Micah 6:8).

KK. "Isaiah again came and reduced them to two : 'Thus says the Lord, (i) Keep justice and (ii) do righteousness' (Isaiah 56:1).

LL. "Amos came and reduced them to a single one, as it is said, 'For thus says the Lord to the house of Israel. Seek Me and live.'

NN. "Habakkuk further came and based them on one, as it is said, 'But the righteous shall live by his faith' (Habakkuk 2:4)."

Bavli Makkot 23b-24a

Living by one's faith should not be misunderstood. Simelai does not mean by "faith" one's personal opinions or beliefs, and he is not commending the individual who stands against the world by reason of personal conviction. By "faith" Simelai understands Habakkuk to mean, "faithfulness," that is, trust in God and loyalty to him, and "the righteous shall live by his faith" means, "by confidence in God's providence." That accords with Amos's "Seek Me and live," and Micah's recommendation to walk humbly with God. Naturally, faithfulness to God yields, also, adherence to justice and mercy, as we have seen earlier, and the actions of those recommended as embodiments of self-abnegation — the ones whose prayers are answered — fit well into the picture before us.

What defines bad character? Once more, we are used to sages' preference for definition through deed. But all together, sages find bad character to embody traits of selfishness and pride and arrogance. These are the attitudes that yield idolatry, fornication, love for gossip, and other forms of self-aggrandizement. Above all else, idolatry, fornication, and murder represent the cardinal sins — the actions by which one manipulates the world round about, trying to govern God, exploit and even eliminate the other:

A. Another matter: "For the earth is filled with violence" (Gen. 6:13):

B. Said R. Levi, "The word for violence refers to idolatry, fornication, and murder.

C. "Idolatry: 'For the earth is filled with violence' (Gen. 6:13).

D. "Fornication: 'The violence done to me and to my flesh be upon Babylonia' (Jer. 51:35). [And the word for 'flesh' refers to incest, as at Lev. 18:6].

E.. "Murder: 'For the violence against the children of Judah, because they have shed innocent blood' (Joel 4:19).

F. "Further, the word for 'violence' stands for its ordinary meaning as well."

Genesis Rabbah XXXI:VI.1

And yet, there is a social vice that matters even more, being commonplace and easy to carry out. When it comes to assessing a person's character, gossip outweighs even idolatry, fornication, and murder:

A. These are four things for the performance of which one is punished in this world, while the principal [i.e., eternal punishment] remains for the world to come, and these are they:

B. [1] idolatrous worship, [2] sexual misbehavior, [3] murder, and [4] gossip, which is worse than all of them [together].

Tosefta-tractate Peah 1:2

The three cardinal sins nonetheless are forgivable, but rejection of the Torah is not, and, once more, we see how the system focuses on its center, whatever topic it treats:

A. R. Huna, R. Jeremiah in the name of R. Samuel bar R. Isaac: "We find that the Holy One, blessed be he, forgave Israel for idolatry, fornication, and murder. [But] for their rejection of the Torah he never forgave them."

B. What is the scriptural basis for that view?

C. It is not written, "Because they practiced idolatry, fornication, and murder," but rather, "And the Lord said, 'Because they have forsaken my Torah.'"

D. Said R. Hiyya bar Ba, "'If they were to forsake me, I should forgive them, for they may yet keep my Torah. For if they should forsake me but keep my Torah, the leaven that is in [the Torah] will bring them closer to me.'"

E. R. Huna said, "Study Torah [even if it is] not for its own sake, for, out of [doing so] not for its own sake, you will come [to study it] for its own sake."

Yerushalmi-tractate Hagigah 1:7/I:3

Why is rejection of the Torah not forgivable? Because the Torah affords knowledge of God and God's will, and rejecting the Torah then brings about all other vices and sins, constituting the ultimate act of arrogance.

Why, then, do people sin, and what is the key to bad character? Sages see two conflicting impulses in the human being, the impulse to do good and the impulse to do evil. That impulse is identified in many passages of the Oral Torah with sexual sins (not sexuality per se). Sages identify the mark of bad character as the dominant trait not only of the gossip but also of the fornicator:

> B. R. Hunia in the name of R. Dosa b. R. Tebet: "Two impulses to do evil did the Holy One, blessed be He, create in his world, the impulse to worship idols, and the impulse to fornicate. The impulse to worship idols has already been eliminated, but the impulse to fornicate still endures.
>
> C. "Said the Holy One, blessed be He, 'Whoever can withstand the impulse to fornicate do I credit as though he had withstood them both.'"
>
> D. Said R. Judah, "The matter may be compared to the case of a snake-charmer who had [two] snakes. He charmed the larger and left the smaller, saying, 'Whoever can withstand this one is certainly credited as though he had withstood them both.'
>
> E. "So the Holy One, blessed be He, eliminated the impulse to worship idols but left the impulse to fornicate. He said, 'Whoever can withstand the impulse to fornicate do I credit as though he had withstood them both.'"
>
> Song of Songs Rabbah XCVI:i.1

The impulse to do evil also bears a good side, so Gen. R. IX:VII.1: Nahman in the name of R. Samuel: "'Behold, it was very good' refers to the impulse to do good. '*And* behold, it was very good' encompasses also the impulse to do evil. And is the impulse to do evil '*very* good'? Indeed so, for if it were not for the impulse to do evil, a man would not build a house, marry a wife, and produce children. So does Solomon say, 'Again I considered all labor and all excelling in work, that is rivalry with his neighbor' (Qoh. 4:4)."

The person of poor character pays a heavy price: that person will never see God. Who are such types? They are scoffers, flatterers, liars, and slanderers:

> G. And said R. Hisda said R. Jeremiah bar Abba, "There are four categories who will not receive the face of the Presence of God:

H. "The categories of scoffers, flatterers, liars, and slanderers."

Bavli-tractate Sanhedrin 11:2 X.4/103a

What these have in common is the use of the power of language for wicked purposes. These are not people who murder, fornicate, or worship idols. These persons will not see God because of things that they say, not do. Once more, we return to sages' basic conviction that attitude and intentionality, reaching expression in language as much as in deed, make all the difference. What is the antidote? It is the shaping of one's attitude and intentionality in the proper way. And how is this done? It is through close study of the Torah, both the written and the oral parts thereof. Everything is captured in a single statement, "God wants the heart," which is amplified by another, "The commandments were given only to purify the heart of humanity." Then who is the person who ought to embody and represent that pure heart that the Torah so highly appreciates? It must be the master of Torah, the sage.

IX.
The Highest Form of Sanctification: Ethical Conduct Embodied in self-sacrifice

The Rabbinic sages paint yet another, and conflicting, picture of the extraordinarily virtuous person. They have the notion that the most ignorant of ignorant persons, who devote their lives to sin, can through a single action accomplish what a life devoted to Torah-study cannot achieve. And that brings us back to our starting point, the merit of the act of selfless love, the act God cannot compel or coerce but craves of humanity. The commandment to love God — "you shall love the Lord your God with all your heart, your soul, and your might" (Deut. 4:9) and to love the other — "you shall love your neighbor as yourself" (Lev. 19:18) meet and form a single statement. It is that to which God aspires for us, but what God cannot impose upon us. God can command love, but not coerce it, favor but not force it. But then God responds to the act of selfless generosity with an act of grace — precisely that act that humanity for its part cannot compel or coerce out of God, cannot cajole from God, but can only beseech.

And no wonder, in sages' account of matters, such a remarkable action done once not only makes up for a dissolute life but in that single moment wins Heaven's perpetual favor. This is the center of the virtue attained through an action that yields zekhut, of sufficient importance to bear repetition, the same story occurring in the entry under Zekhut:

Q. In a dream of R. Abbahu, Mr. Pentakaka ["Five sins"] appeared, who prayed that rain would come, and it rained. R. Abbahu sent and summoned him. He said to him, "What is your trade?"

R. He said to him, "Five sins does that man [I] do every day, [for I am a pimp:] [1] hiring whores, [2] cleaning up the theater, [3] bringing home their garments for washing, [4] dancing, and [4] 'performing' before them."

S. He said to him, "And what sort of decent thing have you ever done?"

T. He said to him, "One day that man [I] was cleaning the theater, and a woman came and stood behind a pillar and cried. I said to her, 'What's with you?' And she said to me, 'That woman's [my] husband is in prison, and I wanted to see what I can do to free him,' so I sold my bed and cover, and I gave the proceeds to her. I said to her, 'Here is your money, free your husband, but do not sin.'"

U. He said to him, "You are worthy of praying and having your prayers answered."

Yerushalmi Taanit 1:4.I

Mr. Five-Sins has done everything sinful that (within sages' imagination) one can do, and, more to the point, he does it every day. What he should do is carry out the commandments, and he should study the Torah every day. So what he has done is what he should not have done, and what he has not done is what he should have done — every day. And yet in a single action, in a moment, everything changes for this unlettered saint.

So the singularity of the act of *zekhut*, which suffices if done only one time, encompasses its power to outweigh a life of sin — again, an act of *zekhut* as the mirror-image and opposite of sin. Here again, the single act of saving a woman from a "fate worse than death" has sufficed. The entire weight of the system points to Torah-study over a lifetime on the part of a man as the realization of virtue. A second look a the story identifies the real hero, who is the heroine, the woman, ready to sell her body to save her husband. So the paradoxes are three: ignorance of the Torah over a lifetime, a woman not a man in a patriarchal system, and a contemplated act of sexual license. The nameless wife, along with Mr. Five-Sins, has carried out an act of grace, to which Heaven, uncoerced and uncompelled, responds with that love in which God so richly abounds for humanity.

I do not think that, within their system, the Rabbinic sages could have underscored their highest aspiration of holiness more vividly than they have done in this total systemic reversal, from learning, maleness, and sexual restraint, to ignorance, femaleness, and sexual license. That underscores what is extraordinary in the systemic proportions: the gift of what God yearns for but cannot coerce, which is, love freely given. The extraordinary person is the one who sacrifices for the other in an act of selfless love — and that can be anybody, at any time, anywhere.

Such a person attains that likeness to God, that holiness, that God yearns for humanity to realize: the ethical imperative of holiness.

2

"THE LORD MADE IT COME LUCKILY TO PASS." THE PRESENT MOMENT IN JUDAIC STUDIES

Donald Harman Akenson
The Rosen Lecture, Queen's University, Kingston, Ontario
October 2001

(1)

It is a privilege to speak with you tonight. The Rosen family has a distinguished record of supporting Jewish studies at Queen's and we all express our gratitude to them. I am personally delighted to be able to talk with my colleagues at Queen's University because the members of the department of religion and the interdisciplinary programme in Jewish studies have been generous to me over the years. And, I should add, admirably tolerant. Coming from the field of Irish studies where verbal viciousness is usually considered a virtue, I cannot tell you how refreshing it has been to be frequently and gently forgiven for my solipsisms and intellectual lapses. The pleasure of being here is heightened because, effectively, my lecture serves as a prologue to the visit of Professor Jacob Neusner. He stands as the colossus in modern Rabbinic studies and it is in large part because of his work that we can have the discussion we are having tonight. The nature of our collective debt to him will become more clear as I speak.

Since I am an historian, that is the voice you are hearing this evening. There are more profound ways to discuss the Judaic material than I am here presenting – literary, philosophical, and theological modes – but one works within one's own small ambit. Historians are usually fascinated by intersections, the moments when persons or forces cross each other's paths in a way that is either causally significant for later events or metonymic of bigger ones.

Tonight's head-text is both. It is from one of the most heroic literary achievements in the English language, William Tyndale's translation into English of the Tanakh in the early sixteenth century, done while he literally was on the run. One of Tyndale's great phrases is this: "The Lord was with Joseph and whatsoever he did, *the Lord made it come luckily to pass.*" [Gen 39:21, 23, spelling modernized]

No cant or pretension there; nor pedantic worry about the concept of luck. It exists.

My central point tonight is that at this moment in Western intellectual history, anyone who has a serious interest in the development of Jewish and Jewish-related texts is a lucky person. We all are: because the availability of authentic early texts is greater than it ever has been in history. Ever: and even if that sounds a large statement, it bears expansion. Namely: because of modern methods of text production, and because of immense achievements in text translation and editing, and because of some good luck among fossickers, each of us can conveniently have available to us more material from the period 200BCE to 600CE, than did even Rashi, Maimonides, or even the Sages of Blessed Memory themselves. "The Lord made it come luckily to pass."

(2)

I once enquired of the great Jacob Neusner if I would be out of line to suggest that probably no more than one person in 100,000 of the world's Jewish population of the present day has read completely the major texts of Rabbinic Judaism. He replied, "No. You'd be correct if you said that in the entire history of Judaism, no more than one in 100,000 *Rabbis* had read all the classical texts."

To me, as a secular historian, that statement is a puzzle that demands attention. Why is it the case that the mainline items of the faith have been incompletely appreciated?

Let us make this a workable historical puzzle. We will deal only with the central items that would receive consensus-inclusion as part of the Rabbinic corpus. (There are other candidates, but these are the lynchpins):

- Mishnah
- Tosefta
- Sifre
- Jerusalem Talmud
- Babylonian Talmud

Most Jews and most Rabbis, throughout the history of Rabbinic Judaism, would not have read these core items. Why?

First, because of a number: 10 million. That is roughly the number of words in this, the basic spine of Rabbinic Judaism.

Second: Immense linguistic difficulty. None of the texts is easy reading, for each is cast largely in the form either of outline-of-argument, or of exegetical commentary on earlier texts, with the very occasional anecdote tucked in. Hard reading: especially in its original form which requires an advanced knowledge of biblical Hebrew, middle Hebrew, Eastern Aramaic, Western Aramaic, and a moderate facility in the Palestinian and Syrian dialects of Greek, and a smattering of medieval French. Not a lot of people have possessed those skills.

Third, Christians. For the first millennium or more after these texts were completed, they were available only in manuscript form. And Christians frequently destroyed sacred Jewish texts. The campaign of the thirteenth century to destroy Jewish literature is notorious but not unique. The result was that it was very difficult for any single spiritual academy or any single Rabbinic master to gain access to the entire corpus.

Fourth, here are some other numbers: dates.

1485
1521
1523
1524
1523

These are the respective dates when the volumes became available in printed forms. Only at that point – and it is late in the history of Rabbinic Judaism – were they available to virtually all serious students.

Yet the base problem remained. The texts were exceedingly difficult and it became the practice to concentrate in Yeshevot upon only the final item in the Rabbinic corpus, the Bavli. That practice continues (although not universally) to this day. Now, to the extent that this is a spiritual decision, made under Rabbinic authority, one cannot question it. Nor can one question the pedagogic strategy of having young students immerse themselves in limited segments of the Bavli. However, at some point, for adults who are curious about the wider aspects of Jewish history, it might be useful to replace the admonition to the young – Now: Go: Study – with a suggestion: Now, why not go and read? Read the whole corpus, so you'll know where the specific components fit. It's what an adult would do with any secular body of literature – survey before swimming – and it should work here.

And now we're at a very touchy point. Here is another set of dates:

- 1933
- 1980
- 1988
- 1993
- 1948

These are the dates when the basic items of Rabbinic Judaism became available in a modern European language – in this case English, the only language (other than modern Hebrew) into which the Rabbinic corpus has been translated.

That most of this front-edge work was done by Professor Neusner will not, I think, surprise you. This, the body of literature which the Jews preserved, and which, in turn, preserved them: why available so late in a vernacular tongue? Why was the overwhelming bulk of the laity locked out of these texts, in the same way that the Roman Catholc church kept the scriptures out of the vernacular as long as possible? I do not know, but except for the Tanakh, no text originally in Hebrew or Aramaic in the Judaic canon reached a foreign language, except Latin, before the nineteenth century. And some early attempts at translation were blocked by religious authorities. For example, a mid-nineteenth century effort at translating the Babylonian Talmud into German was scuttled under pressure by extreme Orthodox leaders. Mostly, however, translations into vernacular languages foundered not on direct opposition, but because those scholars who were expert enough to do the work had no interest in having the texts widely read. There was a sense that translations were vaguely impure. Here, I must recall that my teacher, and later colleague at Yale, Judah Goldin, once rebuked, in his very gentle way, one of his more pretentious colleagues, noting, "by the way, the Hebrew alphabet has only consonants and quite often it is hard to decide how a word is pronounced." Then Professor Goldin stuck the needle in. "It is from the New Testament, which is written in Greek, that we learn that certain Hebrew consonants should be pronounced 'Rabbi.'"

You, however, live in a new era. You are the first generation to have available to you, in highly competent translations, the spine of the faith. Moreover, among these translations are versions that overcome one of the banes of studying this amazing material: the lack of an efficient system of referencing. This new system, developed by Professor Neusner, is slightly controversial, but it should ultimately provide an agreed and precise way of referring to idea units, the way the adoption of the medieval Christian system of versification makes referencing the Tanakh relatively easy.

(3)

"The Lord made it come luckily to pass."

We are doubly lucky because we have been given in our own time not only the glorious Rabbinic corpus in a form any of us can study, but the earth itself has provided a second set of treasures, the Dead Sea Scrolls and related items.

When I mention the Dead Sea Scrolls – a shorthand for material found mostly at Qumran and Masada – you are apt to shrug and I don't blame you. The Dead Sea Scroll industry was one of the most corrupt academic operations of the last century. It took one of the world's great cultural treasure troves and turned it into private chunks of property, with scholars acting just like pirates breaking up a tiara, picking out the best jewels for themselves. Biblical scholars took private control of individual pieces, slowed or embargoed their publication, and sometimes provided for the future lifetime employment of their own graduate students. This has all now passed.

And so too has the miasma that arose in the early days, when, in the late 1940s and early 1950s, first, these hundreds of texts were going to show us what early Christianity was about – there are still a few fanatics on that, but not many. And, then, suddenly, all the texts were declared to belong to one denomination of pre-Destruction Judaism, the Essenes. This was a pretty amazing jump because, in fact, we have not a single identifiable text originating with the late pre-Destruction Pharisees, nor from pre-Destruction Sadducees, nor from the priestly establishment, nor from the Essenes.

But it was convenient to dump them all into the Essene basket. Partially, this was defensive: it isolated the new texts of the pre-Destruction period from what was believed in those days to be the normative line of Jewish history, running in a straight line from the exile, through the priestly establishment and through Pharisaism to Rabbinic Judaism. So it was natural to try to keep the new texts to one side, a category labelled "Essenes."

One does not want to be too harsh here: the early caves made an Essene-hypothesis sensible – as long as it was stated as an hypothesis and then verified or falsified. The trouble is, the Essene hypothesis was never tested by those most able to assay its validity, the group that controlled the Qumran manuscripts. And when manuscripts were found at Masada, it was immediately stated that these were fragments of a branch of the main Essene community based at Khirbet Qumran.

This Essene position was not so much proved, but approved of. It was especially congenial to the French monks who controlled the project as it allowed them to depict a group of Jewish dévotes who had most of the characteristics and virtues of... well... of French monks.

What had been a sensible initial hypothesis – one worth testing – when there were no more than half a dozen texts, simply did not work with the roughly 1,000 manuscripts (many are duplicates, granted) that are now recognized as being represented in the caves. Had the early scholars framed their ideas properly – that is, by requiring positive proof of a tightly defined hypothesis – they would have known by the middle 1950s that they were not dealing entirely with the Essenes. The reason is simple: the fragments cannot be identified with any single group; rather, they form a complex and heterogenous library.

You can prove this for yourself. Get someone to xerox for you four or five copies of the latest complete set of DSS translations. Then rent a gymnasium. Now, as if you are playing solitaire, try to arrange the idea-units found in the fragments in a way that makes them compatible with each other and thus potentially part of a single denominational belief system. It won't work. And no scholar has been able to argue that they all fit together. And if actually pressed together, as one set of beliefs, they would resemble nothing so much as schizophrenic discourse.

What one has in the Qumran and associated caves is not the sacred texts of some single Jewish denomination, but instead a diverse library. This library is made up of texts that bear religious ideas.

Now, the one thing we agree about Judaism is that it is a religion of texts. No texts, no Judaism. No text, no Moses. No text, then Sinai is just a mountain.

So, these being "merely"' religious texts, rather than the membership lists of religio-political parties or artifacts made of stone or iron, is no handicap. The texts tell us what various Jews were thinking in the pre-Destruction era, roughly from the Maccabeans onwards. And the lushness, the vividness, the variety of their thought is impressive, and beyond. They instantiate in detail what Jacob Neusner has long argued: that in the later Second Temple era, if one wishes to be accurate, one speaks not of a single Judaism, but of multiple Judaisms.

We'll come back to that in a moment, but here I should add that the Dead Sea finds are even more productive than they first appear. That is because they contain fragments in Hebrew or in Aramaic of authentic documents that have long been preserved (while being virtually ignored) by Christian archivists. For example, if one looks at the Qumran library, one finds that the non-Biblical texts most often represented are the Book of Enoch and the Book of Jubilees. The DSS fragments not only authenticate documents in Christian keeping that were declared forgeries until 1950 by Jewish authorities, but they allow the expansion of the Qumran fragments by permitting our employing the full versions as preserved (in these two cases) in Ethiopic in the deserts of Africa. I won't push this argument, but some scholars suggest that the DSS can be used as a sort of sampling system: if so, then the Book of Enoch and the Book of Jubilees were, outside the Tanakh, the most-read Jewish religious texts of the late Second Temple era. (I have my reservations about that sampling method.)

However, in any case, there are at least 100 Jewish religious documents now known from the late Second Temple era that were not known or were not recognized as authentic in 1950. If you are willing to put them together with the full Rabbinic corpus, which mostly became accessible in the last fifty years, and fully only within the last decade, then you are at a point where it is possible for you to know as historians more about the ideational character of Judaism in the two centuries before the Destruction and the five centuries thereafter than did anyone – even the most learned of Rabbis – in the dozen or so centuries prior to 1950.

Yes, the Lord is with you, and you are lucky indeed.

However, just as Joseph's luck brought responsibility, so does yours. Obviously, one avoids two extremes: the one is to freeze up and deny that any of this material is of any use, since grandfather knew nothing of it; the alternative is to go off half-cocked and latch on to one segment of the Rabbinic corpus or the Dead Sea Library and to embrace it without paying attention to the entire context of the time and of the many texts in question. A wide angle lens is important here.

And that lens should take into its field of vision not only these new items, but always, centrally, the Tanakh.

Why do I make this obvious point about breadth of perspective? Because the standard story one still hears – so standard that it is repeated without attribution – is based on a two-volume work of George Foot Moore, of 1927 and 1930, entitled *Judaism in the First Centuries of the Christian Era*. Unlike almost all other Christian scholars of his day, Moore paid attention to the post-70 Rabbinic texts. But, unfortunately, to not much else. Moore developed the concept of "normative Judaism." It was a faith of Eretz Israel, not the diaspora, and was essentially Rabbinism writ small, which is to say, Pharisaism. Everything else was deviant – not normative.

Although even at the time of its propounding there were difficulties with the concept of normative Judaism – there was a diaspora, after all, and also non-Pharisaic forms within Eretz Israel. This concept served two groups very well. One of these was the heirs of the Rabbis, for it propelled Rabbinic Judaism back through the messiness of the Second Temple – via Pharisaism, which was declared normative – and thus into the times of the Tanakh and thence to the theophany at Sinai. The other group that really liked it was the Christians. It was used by many of their pastors to say that there was a direct line from Sinai down to the Pharisees and that, at that point, the Yeshua-faith took over.

You notice that both are forms of focus-narrowing by means of linear thinking: history is defined as having a single trajectory and HaShem is required to follow a set of nice straight train tracks.

Well, he just refuses to do so. It's his world, not ours.

If we fix in our mind the fundamental story of the Chosen People as found in the primary text of Judaism – Genesis through Kings – and if we relate to it the millions of new datum points that we now have readily to hand in the full Rabbinic corpus and in the faith-writings of the later Second Temple era, what patterns do we see? Let's consider really big things.

First, we observe that Rabbinic Judaism *seems* to be going off at an unexpected angle. It *seems* to be rejecting the basic traditions of the Tanakh: not on any specific issue, but on the big matter of how truth is communicated. Many of you will know the work of the literary critic Robert Alter. "It is peculiar, and culturally significant," he has written, "that among ancient peoples only Israel should have chosen to cast its sacred national traditions in prose." Of course there is some spectacularly good poetry along the way, but prose carries the burden. And, Alter emphasizes, it is not epic prose, for that is associated with the world of paganism and polytheistic cults, but prose narration.

Prose narration. Compare that first to the Mishnah, in which there is virtually no narration, only legal discussion and some historical description of the now-destroyed Temple. And even in the Bavli, which is the most voluble of the books of the Rabbinic corpus, there are short stories – aggadah – but overwhelmingly Halachah. No prose narration. *Seemingly* the unique and distinctive form of encapsulating and communicating the Jewish faith has been abandoned.

Instead of narrative tales that explain to mankind how God *does* act, one now has thousands of individual cases argued, each of which helps to define how humankind *should* act. These are huge changes from the traditional methods of the Tanakh. At minimum, the primary narrative sections of the Tanakh, which end at 587BCE, and the Rabbinical corpus do not lie on a single straight set of train tracks.

Don't worry: we're not headed for heresy here, but we must go a bit farther into the desert before circling back.

Even more striking is how different the Rabbinic corpus is from the pluralism of belief, from the whirlwind of ideas, that swirled around the Second Temple. At one point the Jerusalem Talmud records the third-century comment of Rabbi Johanan that there had been twenty-four parties of heretics in operation before the Destruction of the Temple. That is a dismissive comment, although probably basically accurate if one replaces the word "heretic" with "parties," "denominations," or "faith groups." The interesting thing is that the Rabbinic corpus pays almost no attention to the late Second Temple era, save to its own antecedents and to the Temple itself. The Rabbinic corpus is immensely self-affirmative and it dismisses with disdainful silence everything in late Second Temple history except its own forebears. The tone is one that you might remember from Henry Fielding's *Tom Jones*. There Parson Thwackum, an insular Anglican priest, discusses religion. "When I mention religion," he says, "I mean the Christian religion: and not only the Christian religion, but the Protestant religion: and not only the Protestant religion, but the Church of England." In other words, Thwackum defines religion as his own narrow branch of Christianity. A parallel exercise is conducted by the Rabbis. The Rabbinic practice of Judaism is the only possible religion and, of course, the only possible Judaism.

But recall the world from which the early Sages had come: the Jerusalem from which Yohannen ben Zakkai had been smuggled in a coffin shortly before the Destruction. It was not a nice, tight world in which all the lines were clearly ruled, like those on a grid map of rural Saskatchewan. It was a world of dust, swirl, blurred definitions; a world of persons of fervent conviction and deep commitment to the path of righteousness who frequently disagreed with one another, sometimes to the point of violence. The Rabbis as spiritual visionaries may have made these complexes of people disappear, but as historians we should not. The reason we should keep them in the historical picture is that they did indeed exist and they will help us to understand the miracle that is Rabbinic Judaism. If the Almighty wants to work through the religious equivalent of biodiversity, who are we to question His wisdom?

And, certainly, the late Second Temple era was one of immense biodiversity within Judaism. (I am intentionally avoiding the vexed question of whether or not there was a common denominator among all the pre-Destruction forms of Judaism and, if so, what it may have been.) When you have time, take a look at the rich array of texts that were circulating in Jerusalem just before the Destruction. Amazing, bewildering variety and flux. (I should remind you that even the Temple was in flux during most of the era, for the building begun by Herod the Great still was under construction in the early '60s of the Common Era.)

What we find are books that are excluded from the Tanakh that explain the origin of Hanukkah (1 and 2 Maccabees); the very popular Book of Jubilees which is nothing less than an alternative Pentateuch; several alternative versions of the Books of Moses, the Apocryphon of Joseph and the Genesis Apocryphon being the most important; corrections or augmentations of the Scriptures found in things such as the Testament of the Twelve Patriarchs, the Book of Noah and several books ascribed to Moses; the Temple Scroll that proposes an entirely new Temple and a new formulation of priestly duties; and there are apocalypses – that is, narratives of the future – of which the Book of Enoch was probably the most widely read.

All this was within Eretz Israel. In diaspora settings, among people who undeniably were Jewish, one has, for example, Philo of Alexandria, an amazingly prolific writer. He produces his own version of the narrative of the Chosen People and argues that Greek philosophy is potentially compatible with the truth of the Jewish religion. In Leontopolis in Egypt there was a temple – not a synagogue, a temple – where sacrifices were conducted. This had its origin in the dismissal of the Zadokite line that traced itself as high priests back to the era of King David, by the Maccabeans. Onias IV, son of the last high priest (who was murdered) sought refuge in Egypt and there was given permission by King Ptolemy Philometer to create a sacrificial site. This diaspora temple could claim a purer priestly genealogy than the Temple in Jerusalem and operated until it was destroyed by Vespasian in 73CE.

One could go on and on, and that is without even mentioning the political movements that swarmed in Eretz Israel, most of which had a religious element as well as a political agenda: for in the Holy Land the two are inseparable.

Whatever we make of any of these individual textual items – and they do deserve our close study – their sum total is clear: the later Second Temple era was a time of whirlwind, of multiple Judaisms, of diverse formulations of the ancient faith. There was no normative Judaism. How this wind would have settled out – cruelly or gently – had the Destruction not occurred is a fascinating counter-factual question.

What did happen was a miracle. A meteor, metaphorically speaking, hit the earth and no species of Judaism could have been expected to survive. The marrow of the several Judaisms was destroyed: the Temple, where the original theophany was daily affirmed, the covenant daily renewed. Gone. Yet the Pharisees were able to survive and to rapidly evolve into a form of Judaism that is vigorous and has been only rarely open to challenge (as by the Karaites in the ninth century).

It is a miracle, certainly. But even miracles have chronicles, which is to say partial explanations.

I think the reason Rabbinic Judaism came through the effects of the Destruction so well is that it was *pre-adapted* to the disaster. This is something often seen in the biological world. A genetic grouping will develop some characteristic that is not especially adaptive in a given context – say a little extra body fat on a mammal – but in the case of a disaster – say a short ice age of the sort that frequently follows big volcanic eruptions – this random pre-adaptation to disaster will be the difference between survival and extinction.

It's luck, but remember the text: "The Lord was with Joseph and whatsoever he did, the Lord made it come luckily to pass." The Pharisees were pre-adapted to a Jewish world in which there was no Temple, because, even before the Destruction, they had been building a form of Judaism in which each house was a temple, each male a priest, each member of the family an acolyte. They practised Temple purity at home. For them, it was a natural step to create an invisible temple to replace the visible one. And there was no reason for them to memorialize all the other rival Judaisms of the recent past.

The Mishnah is their primary monument, the document that makes the invisible Temple eternal and study of Torah the replacement and equal of priestly service in the now-dust Temple of Herod.

The need for clear rules of social and religious purity in such an environment is obvious, and that explains why there is so much Halachah. What it does not explain is why narrative not only was given up by the Rabbis, but was suppressed if it was of recent origin. Here the answer is, I think, that one abandons narrative history when it comes out wrong and for the Jews of 70CE and again of 135, it came out very wrong indeed. According to Yosef Yerushalmi, the ability to write sustained narrative history did not reappear amidst the Jewish intellectual elite until the resurgence of Jewish historical writing in the sixteenth century.

So both secular and divine history can bend, take wild angles, swirl, as well as proceed along nice straight lines. Anyone who lives in the twenty-first century and is sentient should not find that surprising.

(4)

That brings me to now – today – and to two brief observations.

The first is that as a citizen of the Academy (in the broad sense of those who are by profession committed to research and to teaching) I am convinced that we have been shortchanging our students by failure to include some representative portions of the great Rabbinic corpus in our basic instruction in the humanities.

This has been mostly an unconscious decision, dictated in part by the texts being difficult of access until recently, and reinforced by our own cultural blindness. Our students deserve to experience as part of their secular education contact with some of the nimblest minds that have ever conducted logical argumentation. Selected portions of the Babylonian Talmud would be a suitable place to start.

There is more to my suggestion than that, however. As an historian I am unsettled by the instinctive affirmation and glorification of things "Classical" and the equally instinctive denigration of things Semitic. Despite Canadian universities' formal liberation from our British mortmain, collectively we still have pockets of attitude that come right out of the English public school tradition of the pre-Second War era. I once found myself teaching a section of an introductory World Thought course that had on the syllabus undigestible lumps of the writings of Marsillius of Padua and not a word by the sublime Maimonides. That pretty much says it all.

My second today-observation is this. We all read the present like a book. In my reading the present-day situation in the world of the Jewish faith is that it is in a period of whirlwind. Of multiplicity of belief systems. Of frequent re-interpretations. Of searches for the past and of groping for a future. Of fabulous visions and of visionary fables. An amazing time and maybe a frightening time.

Nothing is certain, except that the Almighty can handle things anyway He wishes, from sustaining complexity to simplifying ruthlessly.

It's not our choice.

So, walk with the Lord. And be lucky.

3

UNCOVERING THE PLOTS: THE IMAGE OF RABBI SHIMON BAR YOHAI

HERBERT W. BASSER
QUEEN'S UNIVERSITY

Professor Jacob Neusner honors Queen's University and the Queen's Theological College in delivering the Mathers lecture of 2001. His theme deals with holiness and "holier than thou." To commemorate his visit he has suggested that those who do research in the areas of Jewish texts at Queen's contribute to a volume marking the occasion of his lecture. While Professor Neusner is invited to offer lectures, literally hundreds of times over, the present volume marks a distinct and unique recognition of the Queen's visit. I am honored to be part of this occasion, having been in Queen's Religious Studies Department some 22 years on the one hand and having been a professional associate of Professor Neusner for most of those years on the other. Ironically, Religious Studies at Queen's offers not a single course in the teachings of Judaism (although the idea of a chair of Jewish Studies that I first proposed in the early 1980's has come to fruition with the result that Jewish Studies courses are taught in a few departments now, it is currently based in History, but none are taught in Religious Studies). Since I have been long interested in the development of forms of Jewish thought throughout the ages and have published some modest offerings in this subject, this volume presents me with a rare opportunity of participating in a thoroughly Judaic academic exercise as a direct result of my presence at Queen's. I am grateful he has invited me to contribute some thoughts in this volume. In conjunction with Professor Neusner's presentation I examine here the talmudic treatments of the deeds of Rabbi Shimon bar Yohai, the arch example of a Rabbi well known for his "holier than thou" attitudes. The complexity of the development of the stories allows us to see that the talmudic reporters suggest sometimes such "pious" attitudes are useful and sometimes they can destroy the world. A version of the story introduces Rabbi Yosi, the most tolerant and progressive of the early Rabbis, and I include a short appendix on the effect of his views throughout the ages.

1. State of recent research on the b Yohai tales.

In this paper we explore the character portrayal of Rabbi Shimon bar Yohai by comparing Jewish Palestinian and Babylonian talmudic sources. Our purpose is to understand features of the story that have presented dilemmas to most readers and in so doing expose the points of view of the Rabbis towards Roman culture. What we deal with is the conscious composition of pieces of rabbinic folklore woven through the threads of biblical exegesis. Two recent works on these stories merit discussion at the outset and a third at a later point in the paper. In a recent article, Ben-Zion Rosenfeld[1] deals with the rabbinic sources discussing Rabbi Shimon bar Yohai. He finds that the characterization of him as a pious sage fits a historical type that flourished in the second century CE (140-170). He accepts the report that Rabbi Shimon was the teacher of Rabbi Judah, the reputed redactor of the Mishnah. It was Rabbi Shimon above all others who reconstituted the religious leadership of The Sages in the Galilee in the aftermath of the failed Bar Kochba revolt. Rosenfeld notes a plethora of talmudic sources, which show Shimon to be a wonder-worker if not a magician.[2] His analysis of the stories we deal with is cogent and useful.[3] His work dispels some previous claims by scholars like Graetz and Urbach that Rabbi Shimon bar Yohai's reputation as a magician is the product of medieval mystics, and is not warranted by a reading of the materials of late antiquity.[4]

Lee Levine's earlier work deserves thorough discussion.[5] Since we deal with stories in which Rabbi Shimon bar Yohai hides in a cave for thirteen years and emerges as a wonder-worker who cleanses Tiberias of its stigma as a city built on graveyards (making it difficult for priests or others who kept purity laws beyond the measure of the law to live there), we are fascinated to learn that there is a Greek cycle of legends with this very motif. A collections of legends found in various sources speak of how Epimenides, the Cretan philosopher of the sixth century BCE, lived (slept) in a cave for fifty-seven years, and because he had the reputation of a miracle-worker when he emerged was called upon to cleanse Athens of its corpses after the city had been devastated by a plague. After using various methods he was able to remove the corpses. Levine thanks Morton Smith for drawing his attention to the striking resemblance which might lead us to consider that perhaps Rabbi Shimon really did purify Tiberias and the Epimendes story was assimilated in the manner that legends get transferred into the telling of cross-cultural stories. Levine thinks the rabbinic story is meant to show the supremacy of Tiberias as the city of Rabbi Shimon, as it competed with Sepphoris. Both he and Rosenfeld see Rabbi Shimon as the ideal hero in these dream-like stories.

Levine finds the more original version of the stories in that found in Genesis Rabba 79. In a synoptic presentation he compares the sources in Genesis Rabba, Pesikta deRav Kahana and Midrash Esther Rabba where he traces the embellishments through to what he sees as the composite version of the Yerushalmi. He suspects the miraculous features are joined to natural feats in some of our versions to explain the same events because the more fantastic features were added later. He then sees the latest version, that of the Babylonian Talmud, to be full of later embellishments and interpolations which he deals with in a variety of ways. Rosenfeld also notes some of the rhetorical features but adds little to the discussions of Levine.[6]

2. Introduction to disquieting talmudic stories

In my opinion the stories fit a genre, which were constructed to agitate us, and purposely create tensions with no simple solutions, although it does take a view on some matters. Rather than see the versions in opposition to each other through clumsy editing I suspect the growth of these stories have a purpose which as of yet no one has discussed satisfactorily. Interpolations are rarely meant to contradict a story but aim to explain the source that lay before the interpolator. Thus interpolation is a form of commentary and footnoting. In our case the interpolations, I now argue, are meant to explain the tension between the techniques of miracle-working and rabbinic legal process to make decisions. As Rosenfeld rightly notes no one but Rabbi Shimon mixed the two categories to the extent he did. Babylonian Talmud interpolates materials to show that Rabbi Phineas ben Yair, the great wonder-worker, could not match Rabbi Shimon's halachic acuity. Also, the scenes of Rabbi Shimon working quasi-magic to purify the city is juxtaposed to more rational methods in both Jewish Palestinian and Babylonian sources. The tension between the two methods is left with the reader until the end settles the matter: in any event, Rabbis have power through democratic processes to sustain any type of procedure they wish. Genesis Rabba takes the view that he did nothing which he could not have done using halachic sources, even if we discount the magic. Heretics and even scribes who oppose rabbinic decision making processes are severely punished in these stories. The magic and legal stand in creative tension in these stories but not in opposition as we might think they should. Likewise the Babylonian addition of a debate over the value of Roman civilization is introduced (based on earlier literary formulations) not only to explain why Rabbi Shimon had to hide but also to highlight the tension in disparaging Rome and appreciating it at the same time. These tensions are not introduced as departures from the original stories but as explanatory enhancements to a basic story that was understood to have these elements implicitly. Finally the additions where Rabbi Shimon is told from heaven that his zeal for Torah study is destructive is meant to contrast with his zeal for upholding majority legal processes as required by Rabbinic law. Charismatic wonder workers have no authority to undermine the Jewish legal process. And they have no right to force their pietistic ideals on others. What they do have is the right to zeal for rabbinic democracy. It seems to me that the additions to the story are meant to express these polarities. As such these stories stand in tension with other stories that use the same motifs and language to disparage Rome. Furthermore, the stories show us that one ought to be cautious and fearful to criticize, or even speak to, wonder-workers and holy men. This particular view of the image of Rabbi Shimon's exploits has not been explored adequately before.

We begin our discussion with this story from Babylonian Talmud, Avodah Zarah 18a:

Our Rabbis taught the following in a *baraita.*

> When Rabbi Yosi ben Kisma fell ill Rabbi Haninah ben Tradyon went to visit him. He said to him, "Haninah my brother, do you not know that this nation [of Rome] rules through the will of Heaven? Consider that they destroyed His Temple and burned His Sanctuary and killed His devout and destroyed his blessed ones. Yet, this nation continues to endure. Now I have heard about you that [in defiance of Rome] you sit and study Torah and teach throngs publicly with a scroll of the Torah in your lap."
>
> He said to him, "They will have mercy on me through the will of Heaven.
>
> He replied, "I gave you a sound argument and you retort that they will have mercy through the will of Heaven! I would be amazed if they do not burn you and your Torah scroll in a fire.
>
> He said to him, "Rabbi, what else can I do to enter the next world?"
>
> He said to him, "Have not opportunities for good deeds come your way?"
>
> He replied, "My own money for celebrating Purim inadvertently got mixed into charity funds and I gave everything to the poor."
>
> He said to him, "If so, may my portion be as yours and my lot be as yours."
>
> It was told that only a few days later Rabbi Yosi ben Kisma died and all the nobles of Rome went to his funeral and eulogized him with great acclaim.[7] Upon their return they discovered Rabbi Hanina ben Tradyon was sitting and studying Torah and teaching throngs publicly. A Torah scroll was in his lap. They took him and wrapped him in the Torah scroll and surrounded him with piles of wool and set them on fire... a heavenly voice went out and said: "Hanina ben Tradyon... is set for the next world."[8]

I have discussed the essential rhetorical features of this story elsewhere to illustrate the way that rabbinic stories develop out of kernels of fact as embellished by scriptural exegesis and the harmonizing of variants of the same story.[9]

Michael Chernick, writing after Rosenfeld and Levine, has penned a "forty page" article to expound the stories of Rabbi Shimon bar Yohai and the history of interpretation surrounding them.[10] He has translated the materials,[11] noted bibliography,[12] and offered an interesting analysis of how the story addressed objectives appropriate to talmudic times,[13] and then was reinterpreted to meet purposes[14] specific to medieval times,[15] early modern and modern times. To accomplish this latter item, Chernick himself reduces the story to a kind of social, psycho-analytic, literary kind of symbolic discourse to show how the story directs the reader to consider the internal disharmony between physicality and spirituality, natural space and sacred space, commonplace and Torah all in the psyche of a devout Rabbi and his broad-minded alter-ego critics.[16] All in all, Chernick's striking reading of the Babylonian version for all its play and stretch, here and there will meet flush with the plane of the story only at select points. This impressive *tour de force* does not convince that the story was ever meant to be read that way by its original authors but in post-modern readings that is of no consequence.[17] Thus, such aesthetic readings are not open to pedantic criticisms[18] but to acceptance or rejection by the reader.

What I, in contrast, stress in the Babylonian version is how the tale develops the ambivalence of Rabbinic policies to Rome as an occupying force, submissive attitudes on one side but hostile ones on the other. Rome is capable of endearing those who accommodate themselves to their values on the one hand and of acting brutally to those who do not. Is Rome enforcing the divine will or opposing it? That problem remains unanswered. Chernick pushes Rabbi Yosi out of the picture but I think his position is a central one. But the story has more to say than just that and the Babylonian introduction only reflects the inherited ambiguity of the story as a whole. The central motif of the stories as a whole is to weigh the miraculous elements against the rational, the charismatic against the legal, the tolerant against the intolerant. The story poses problems and questions upholding the charismatic only when it is ratified by the natural. Thus, in the Palestinian versions Yohai deduces from a heavenly voice that the coast is clear, he really does not venture out of his cave until he checks out if things have really become quiet. Furthermore, he uses magic to locate corpses but (in Babylonian sources finds a rational way to proceed and in the Palestinian ones he claims to have legal precedents even if he dreamt certain aspects) needs a court to certify what he has done. At this point the sources tell us it is proper to object to charismatic pronouncements but not to court sanctioned ones. While the stories are imbued with magical overtones they uphold the authority of rabbinic bodies to certify "grave" leniency.

3. Rabbi Shimon b. Yohai: The Babylonian view.

We will now consider the major features of the Shimon bar Yohai story as told by the Babylonian Talmud. Here we find the same tension that we found above between ben Kisma and ben Tradyon but this time between ben Ilai and bar Yohai. What should be the proper response to Roman power: admiration, accommodation or condemnation, defiance. However, unlike other presentations of the debate, another voice is offered here as well, that of endorsing the right of individuals to choose either way. There can be no settling of the issue. The analysis of the following cycle of highly complex stories may open our eyes to these attitudes of the Rabbis towards zealotry, resistance and opposition to Rome on the one hand or to peaceful co-existence, accommodation and submission on the other.

Babylonian Talmud Shabbat 33b

I. And how did Rabbi Yehudah get the title "First Speaker Everywhere"?[19]

Once Rabbi Yehudah and Rabbi Yosi and Rabbi Shimon were sitting in a study session[20] and Rabbi Yehudah son of Gerim was seated nearby. Rabbi Yehudah spoke, "How wonderful are the works [in the Land of Israel] of the Romans! 1. They organize markets. 2. They erect bridges. 3. They build bathhouses." Rabbi Yosi remained silent. Rabbi Shimon said, "Everything they do they do only for their own ambitions.[21] 1. They organize markets so they can place brothels in them; 2. bath houses so they can preen themselves; 3. bridges to collect tolls from them."

II. Rabbi Yehudah ben Gerim[22] went and repeated these things and it was overheard by the Romans who decreed (a) "Yehudah [son of Ilai] who acclaimed [*ilah*] shall be elevated [*yitaleh*—Rashi: to the post of "First Speaker Everywhere"].[23] (b) Yosi who remained silent shall be banished to Sepphoris.[24] (c) Shimon who criticized shall be killed."[25]

III. He and his son fled to the study house. His wife brought him food and water and they ate. As the decree against him became harsher he said to his son, "Since women break easily she may be tortured and give us away." They went to hide in a cave. A miracle occurred and a carob tree and water-well were created. They took off their clothes and they lived up to their necks in sand. The whole day they recited texts. At the time of prayer—they would dress, cover themselves and pray and then they would remove their clothes again so these would not wear out.

They had been living twelve years in the cave when Elijah came and stood at the entrance of the cave.[26] "Is there anyone who will inform bar Yohai that the king of Rome has died and his decree has been voided?"

IV. They went out and saw a man who was clearing and planting. He said, "How dare you leave eternal life and occupy yourself with temporal life." Everywhere that they cast their glances was immediately burned up. A heavenly voice came out and said to them, "Have you come out only to destroy my world! Go back to your cave."

They went back and lived there for twelve months. They said, "The judgment of the wicked in Gehenna is 12 months!"

V. A heavenly voice came out and said to leave the cave. They left. Whatever damage Rabbi Elazar inflicted, Rabbi Shimon restored. He said, "My son it is enough for the world that we study Torah. At the close of the Sabbath eve they saw a certain elder who had picked two bundles of myrtle and he was rushing at twilight. They asked him, " What are these for?"

He answered, "To honor the Sabbath."

"But why not use just one?"

"The one symbolizes the positive commandment to 'celebrate the Sabbath day,' (Exodus 20:8) while the other symbolizes the negative commandment to 'solemnize the Sabbath day.' (Deuteronomy 5:12).

He said to his son, "See how dear the commandments are to Israel!" And he calmed down.

VI. Rabbi Phineas ben Yair, his son-in-law[27] heard of their whereabouts and went to meet them. He took him into the baths. He (ben Yair) was smoothing his skin and noted he had crevices in his body, and he began to cry so that his tears dripped and exacerbated the wounds.

He said to him, "Woe is me that I see you in such condition."

He replied, "You should be happy to see me such. Had you not seen me such you would not have found me so learned."

Formerly when Rabbi Shimon bar Yohai would encounter a difficulty Rabbi Phineas ben Yair would offer thirteen solutions, while now if Rabbi Phineas ben Yair raised a difficulty Rabbi Shimon bar Yohai offered twenty-four solutions.

VII. He said, "Since I have been saved through a miracle I must go and contribute something."[28]

> It is written, "And Jacob arrived whole at the city of Shechem (Gen 13:18)."[29]
>
> —Rav related a tradition that it meant whole physically, whole financially, whole spiritually (literally: in his Torah).[30]
>
> And he YXN the face of the city (Gen 13:18).
>
> —Rav related a tradition that he established their own currency for them. Shmuel related a tradition that he established marketplaces for them. Rabbi Yohanan[31] related a tradition that it meant he established bathhouses for them.[32]

VIII. Rabbi Shimon bar Yohai said, "There should be something I can contribute for them."

They said to him, "There is a place where there is a presumption of impurity and the priests do not have an easy tine getting around it."[33]

IX. He said, "Is there anyone who knows if there is any area here that has a presumption of being a clean area."[34]

A certain elder said to him, "Here ben Zacchai[35] cut up[36] *tormosin*-beans of *trumah*."[37]

> He did likewise.[38] Wherever it was soft he purified it, wherever it was hard he marked it as impure.[39]
>
> That (a) certain elder said, "Bar Yohai has decreed [ergo] the cemetery is pure!"
>
> X. He said to him, "If you had not been with us, or even if you had been with us but not voted with us, you would be speaking acceptably. But now that you were both with us and voted with us [yet oppose our ruling] people will complain, 'Whores primp each other! Should not scholars support the decisions of their colleagues.'" He looked at him with his eyes and he died. Then he went out into the market and saw Yehudah ben Gerim.[40] He said, "Is that man still alive!" He looked at him with his eyes and he became a pile of bones.[41]

This story (Part I) which explains the reason for the flight of Shimon exists nowhere else in rabbinic literature although the rest of the story of the flight of Rabbi Shimon is indeed found in Yerushalmi Shevi'it 7:1 (end). From some Palestinian version or other the story found its way into many midrashic compilations such as Bereishit Rabba 79. Apparently a version (more likely several versions) was carried to Babylonia and spread there. The Babylonian version, in its current talmudic setting, is meant to explain how it is that Rabbi Yehudah is called "First Speaker Everywhere." But the passage does not explicitly do that. That question seems to be a literary ploy to introduce the tale of Rabbi Shimon. The story is very problematic, disturbing even, in many ways. Rabbi Yehudah ben Gerim plays the role of unwitting informant. He is painted in Moed Katan 9b as a great sage, the student of Rabbi Shimon bar Yohai, and the chosen master for his sons. The ending of the Shimon story that has Shimon do away with him is so bizarre that the Tosafists did not want to incorporate this part of the story into their talmudic readings. Shimon turns ben Gerim into a pile of bones at the end. Nevertheless, that is part of the tale. What is the point of preserving the saga?

4. Sources used by the Babylonians: an evaluation

Babylonian Talmud Shabbat exposes a current debate that must have developed around the exegesis of Jacob's benefiting the city of Shechem. We will find echoes of this story in other places where the characters are not Yehudah and Shimon but Satan and Michael, Rome and the Almighty. The undercurrent is the question, "To what extent did one have to acknowledge the modernizing of Jewish life as a benefit and feel indebted to non-Jews?" That tension is subtly alluded to in the primary tradition of Shimon bar Yohai's hiding from persecution both in the Babylonian and Yersuhalmi Talmuds. The theme of the story shows us Shimon's view of acknowledging divine grace. While Jacob was said to have benefited the idolaters of Shechem, Shimon bar Yohai is noted to have benefited the priests of Tiberias. We will determine that there were two opposing views of larger gentile society and its contributions of health, transportation, defense, and mercantile markets to Jewish society. The following discussion of the matter has not yet been entertained in current scholarship.

In Babylonian Talmud, Avodah Zarah 2b the Romans themselves claim they were good to the Jews. They use phrases similar to that attributed to Yehudah above. The Romans say, "We erect many bridges; we conquer many cities; we make many wars. We do it all for Israel so they may learn Torah." Then God answers in the language (attributed to Shimon above), "Everything you do, you do only for your own ambitions. you erect bridges to collect tolls from them; conquer cities to get work-gangs; the wars are My doing."

In Wertheimer's *Batei Midrashot* vol 2, "Midrash Aleph-Bet" ch 6 (see the section titled "tractate Satan") we find:[42]

> In the future Samael will reply to God, "Everything I did, did I not do for their benefit so they could study Torah and perform good deeds! Moreover, I erected bridges and bath houses and I amassed silver and gold in the world so the human race might have effective commerce." Then Michael was stayed by his words until God called to him, "Why do you flee?"—Michael responded (to Samael)..."You common fool, everything you did was for your own ambitions: the bridges you erected were to collect taxes each day and the bath houses were to preen yourselves. In the future God will respond to Samael's claim of the commercial benefit of amassing money... "Mine is the silver and Mine is the gold (Haggai 2:8)."

As in Avodah Zarah 2b the excuse is given that Rome was motivated to build so Israel could study Torah. The only common item among all these sources is "the bridges." "Midrash Aleph-bet" and Babylonian Talmud Shabbat 33b also share the bathhouse item in addition.

We recollect that the Rabbis believed Jacob himself had contributed these very items to Canaanite society in recognition of his good fortune. To follow through in the midrashic mode of parsing the Shimon story, we locate the theme (Shabbat 33b) of section II above in Babylonian Talmud, Sotah 11a or Sanhedrin 106a:

> Rabbi Hiyya bar Abba related that Rabbi Simaye (in Exodus Rabba 1:9: Rabbi Symon) said—three were involved in approving Pharaoh's counsel (to drown the baby boy Israelites). These are they: Bilaam, Job and Jethro. A. Bilaam who praised the counsel was killed; B. Job who remained silent was judged with afflictions—and C. Jethro who fled merited that his descendents sat in the hewn chamber of the Sanhedrin.

Apparently Jethro had condemned Pharaoh's idea to kill the baby Israelites and then he escaped. The text is not explicitly clear why he had to flee. That supposition has to be read into the text but does not require a huge stretch. The version of *Otzar Midrashim* (J.D. Eisenstein, vol 2), "Rabbenu haKadosh" was originally copied from a Yemenite manuscript. It seems to preserve a more original reading:

> Three who were involved in Pharaoh's counsel—Bilaam, Job and Jethro: Bilaam who praised the counsel was killed; Job who remained silent was afflicted, Jethro who fled was elevated (*nitaleh*).

The word "nitaleh" in the text of *Rabbenu haKadosh* is arguably the more original reading. Certainly it is true that the *midrashim* preserve the reading of the Babylonian Talmud but that is not unusual since its readings were better known. (The version in Exodus Rabba 27:6 is curious in that it refers to Amalek in the group of Pharaoh's councillors.) What is most surprising is that Shabbat 33b refers to *yitaleh* in the future (he will be elevated) since the Romans were ordering what will transpire. Yehudah *ben Ilai ila* (that is, he praised Rome and was elevated—*nitaleh*). *The Rabbenu haKadosh* version of Pharaoh's councillors mentions "nitaleh" in the past (Jethro condemned and was elevated) since the narrator tells us what transpired at the end of it all. Otherwise the texts resonate together, not without considerable irony.

Let us consider Shabbat 33b sec B in its details: (a) "Yehudah who acclaimed shall be acclaimed (implying in the artificial context of the story that he is given the privilege of "First Speaker Everywhere"); (b) Yosi who remained silent shall be banished to Sepphoris; (c) Shimon who criticized shall be killed. He and his son fled..." The results are the precise inverse of the Pharaoh story. Yehudah who praised is elevated, not punished; Yosi, who was silent, has a mysterious punishment of banishment and Shimon is forced to flee for his life. Both story formats are set up in comparable style although the situations are not at all analogous.

In Shabbat 33b Rabbi Yehudah (the Bilaam counterpart who praises Israel's enemies) is not killed—he is elevated. Yosi (the Joban figure) is banished. Shimon (the Jethro figure) has to flee and hide. In the Pharaoh story the ending is that the one who fled is elevated by God, the one who praised (intrigued) is killed by divine decree, the silent one undergoes forms of suffering.

It must have been that the midrashic view of Pharaoh's counselors intended to show that Jews who saw value in Rome were little less than Bilaams. The author of section II above turns that view around for greater consideration. Correctly, the story has been used by the medieval decisors of Jewish law to permit praising gentile societies and allowing monarchs to appoint Rabbis to authoritative posts.[43] We now discover there are two distinct views of the Babylonian Talmud towards Rome. One view suggests Rome deserves praise for their bettering of society; another suggests they deserve condemnation. The third view is Rabbi Yosi's. Rabbi Yosi has always been seen as the liberal and pluralist. He accords equal favor to both views and will not judge between them.[44]

4. Rabbi Shimon b Yohai: the Palestinian view

We now consider the Talmud Yerushalmi's view of the matter. This version of the story is quite strange as it does not provide any clue as to why Rabbi Shimon hid in a cave save that certain people were pursuing him like one hunts a bird. The Yerushalmi-type story exists in several versions; the version of Pesikta deRav Kahana 11:17 begins with "dilemma" (Yerushalmi's term for introducing a story) and we will argue the midrashic reading in a few places is better than the Leiden MS reading of the Yerushalmi preserved in our printed editions. There are some traces that the Palestinian version originally spoke of Rabbi Shimon and his son Elazar although the story before us speaks only of Rabbi Shimon.[45] The Yerushalmi's story is attached to *Mishnah Shevi'it 9:1* concerning what spontaneous growths may be eaten on the seventh year of the sabbatical cycles: **Rabbi Shimon says: All wild growths are permitted except for the wild growth of cabbage. And the Sages say: All wild growths are forbidden.**

Yerushalmi Shevi'it 9:1

A

Rabbi Shimon[46] was passing[47] through on the Sabbatical year and saw a man reaping [unpremeditated growths]. He said to him: "Is this not forbidden? Are these not unpremeditated growths?" He replied: "Are you not the one who permits such?"

He responded: "But did not my colleagues argue against me!"[48] He applied the verse to him, "Concerning the one who breaches a fence, a snake bites him" (Kohelet 10:8) and that is exactly what happened to him.[49]

[This story is absent in Babylonian Talmud]

B

[A story:] Rabbi Shimon bar Yohai [and Rabbi Elazar his son][50] made their hiding places[51] in a cave [at Beqa] for thirteen years.[52] [They ate] in the cave carobs of *trumah*[53] until their flesh became scaly.[54]

[Babylonian Talmud has a carob tree and water well springing up miraculously as the two are buried up to their necks (naked to preserve their clothes) studying Torah all day, except to pray.]

After twelve years he said, "Should not I go to find out some information about the world." He went out and was sitting at the mouth of the cave when he saw a hunter of birds spread a trap [to catch birds]. [When this one spread it for the first time] he heard a heavenly voice saying *demos*, "reprieved!" and the bird escaped. [When He spread the net for a second time he heard a heavenly voice say *spekula*, "sentenced," and the bird was caught.] He thought—if a mere bird, unless heaven will it, cannot be trapped—how much more a man cannot be trapped. [Must we stay here!] When he saw [heard] the world around was tranquil he said, "Let us go down to inspect the—*demosin*—baths of Tiberias."

[In the version of the Babylonian Talmud we recall, he hears Elijah at the entrance announcing all is clear and he can emerge. They see a man working his field, and not studying, in their rage they burn him with their looks. A heavenly voice criticizes them and they return to the cave for another year. When they come out Rabbi Elazar continues to wipe out people not studying but Rabbi Shimon cures them and notes that if he and Elazar were the only ones studying Torah that would suffice. They then see how the Jews beautify the Sabbath with myrtle and both are calmed. He meets his relative Phineas ben Yair who removes the scales from his skin in the baths and the latter is amazed how bar Yohai can solve any problem he poses in numerous ways.]

C

He said [They said], "We should go and do something to better the world [to acknowledge our gratitude] like our ancestors used to do."[56]

> His point was taken from the verse, which said "And Jacob YXN the face of the city (Genesis13:18)." On such occasions[57] they would make booths[58] for selling in the market [cheaply].[59]
>
> He said [They said], "Let us purify[60] Tiberias. He took *Tormosin*-beans and cut them up and scattered them [in the marketplace] and wherever there was a dead body it floated up and he took it away.[61]

[We recall that in the Babylonian Talmud version we noted that Jacob benefited the city from which he derived assistance. There are three versions of this *midrash* which declare what Jacob did for Shechem: 1) established currency, 2) marketplaces, 3) baths for the people of Shechem. Since bar Yohai realized he has had a miraculous experience he decided to improve Tiberias so that priests once again could traverse the city and not worry about plausible impurities. An old man showed him where ben Zacchai or ben Azzai, had, years ago, cut up *tormosin*-beans that had sanctity. He thus gave evidence that indicated that corpses had not polluted this specific area. Rabbi Shimon realized ben Zacchai (or ben Azzai) had determined the area was pure and proceeded in like manner. Bar Yohai marked out all the hard spots and declared them pure, apparently with the consent of a court.]

D

From above a Cuthean (Christian or Samaritan) was watching the events.[62] He thought, "Should not I go and have sport[63] with this sage of the Jews. [What did he do?] He took a corpse and hid it[64] in a place [market] that the Rabbi had already cleansed of corpses.

He confronted Rabbi Shimon bar Yohai. He said to him: "You did not cleanse this certain place [did you cleanse this certain place? He said, "Yes!"]. Come and I will get it out for you from there.

[He said: "Go and show me."] Rabbi Shimon bar Yohai saw through the Holy Spirit that he had put it there himself. He said: "I decree upon you that those above be able to descend and those below able to rise above[65] and that is exactly what happened to him.

[This story is absent in the Babylonian Talmud]

E

While he was passing [the synagogue of] Magdala[66] he heard the voice [of Nicae] the scholar [of Magdala] saying—so has bar Yohai purified Tiberias![67]

He said: May misfortune befall me if I did not hear[68] that Tiberias would indeed in the future be purified.[69] [Were you not counted with those who voted in favor of this?][70] Yet, even you did not believe![71] Immediately, [He raised his eyes and looked at him and] he became a pile of bones.[72]

[According to the Babylonian Talmud, an elder (the same or another) asked him if Tiberias had really been purified according to the law. Bar Yohai replies that the elder had been part of the court deciding to permit it. He could have excused his comment had he not voted the way he did (Babylonian reading: *nmnyt* (counted)/ Yerushalmi: *hmnym* (believed), Pesikta deRav Kahana: *myn hmnyan* ("in the count," Yerushalmi's source likely read *mnyn* (count) and was altered (*hmnym*) to accord with the magic tenor of the story.) He remarked that even whores primp each other and so for sure scholars should support the decisions of their colleagues. He looked at him with his eyes and he died. When he saw Yehudah ben Gerim he looked at him and he became a pile of bones.]

5. Evaluating and comparing sources

In the midrashic sources, except the Yerushalmi version presented above, the story of Rabbi Shimon's confrontation with the cabbage picker comes at the end of Shimon's emergence from the cave and adventures in Tiberias. It is most cogent to think the editor of the Yerushalmi placed the cabbage story first, reversing the order of the stories, since it is directly connected with the Mishnah. However, in the *midrashim*, the story is featured first because it illustrates how Rabbi Shimon acted in accordance with the *midrashim* to Genesis 13:18. On reaching Shechem after a period of flight from Esau, Jacob appreciated the city's shelter and offered his talents to benefit its inhabitants. In Genesis Rabba 79 Rabbi Elazar says to his father that just as the baths of Tiberias have cleansed them, so they should cleanse Tiberias:

> And he *YXN* the face of the city (Gen 13:18). This means he bestowed gratitude on the "visage" in the city; that is, he began to send them[73] gifts. Another interpretation: And he *YXN* the "visage" of the city; that is, he began to erect booths and sell cheaply. This fits what is said, "A person should bestow favor on a place from which he derived benefit." *(HNYH)*

The last line indicates that we learn from Jacob's actions that one should acknowledge the benefits one derives from a place. The story of Rabbi Shimon's adventures is attached to the *midrashim* because this saying occurs in the Rabbi Shimon story. The protagonists make that statement explicitly in many versions of Genesis Rabba 79. It is absent in some manuscript traditions. However, Theodor-Albeck's (*Bereishit Rabba* p. 941) apparatus and notes indicate the reading is found in both Ashkenazic and Yemenite versions of Genesis Rabba. That indicates it to be an original reading. Also it is found in the parallel *midrashim* texts of Kohelet Rabba and Pesikta deRav Kahanna. This story is integral to the *midrashim* because the story itself illustrates the saying ("A person should bestow favor on a place from which he derived benefit") that is attached to this *midrashim.* It would seem that the editor of Genesis Rabba used a story known to the editor of Yerushalmi Shevi'it but he did not take it from the Yersuhalmi. Likewise we have to note that Genesis Rabba 84:13 derives a lesson from scripture's report: A person must investigate the welfare of any item from which he derives benefit.

The *midrashim* on Genesis 13:18 are cited parenthetically by the editor of the Babylonian Talmud Shabbat 33b. He digresses from his story of Rabbi Shimon's decision to benefit the people of Tiberias by telling us that three versions of the *midrashim* exist. That of Rav, that of Shmuel, that of Rabbi Yohanan. It is Shmuel's version that seems to be known to the Yerushalmi. Rav said Jacob minted coins for them, Shmuel said Jacob set up a market for them, Rabbi Yohanan mentioned Jacob set up bathhouses for them.

We now come to evaluate the development of the versions. It is difficult to know for certain if the Babylonian Talmud has added its own piece to introduce the story or reworked an original Palestinian tradition which is no longer extant. The pieces by which this introduction is put together are easily discovered if we see it as later than the first generation of Amoraim.

The art by which this Babylonian introduction reverses the form of firm traditions might suggest the author operated in a mode to puzzle us. Is Rabbi Yehudah like Satan to praise Rome, is he like Bilaam who praised Pharaoh's plan to kill the Israelite children? The Talmud cites the traditions of the pieces in the names of sages who flourished around the year 225. Hence the introduction which uses the form of these *midrashim* likely dates to a period later than 225 CE. Yet the Babylonian Talmud's introduction to the Shimon story is offered by the editor to artificially solve a question (how did a certain rabbi get his honorific?). The story does not really address this issue unless we read into it a good deal and force matters. The editor of the pericope wanted us to do just that. The conclusion must be that the Babylonian Talmud piece is not original to its setting and has been borrowed from elsewhere. It is therefore earlier than the close of the Talmud but later than 225 CE.

What date can we give to the rest of the story? The Palestinian sources lack a beginning and the story begins after Rabbi Shimon is in hiding. The two talmudic versions agree about a story in which Rabbi Shimon bar Yohai emerges from hiding in a cave for thirteen years and goes to Tiberias to purify it from corpse impurity. These Talmuds contain similar stories that diverge in detail but intersect at five important points:[74] Rabbi Shimon bar Yohai 1) hid in a cave for 13 years; 2) after he left the cave he had a bath in a major city; 3) we hear a *midrash* about Jacob repairing Shechem; 4) he released the city from its status of ritual pollution allowing priests to enter and live there; 5) a sage criticized him and he miraculously executed him (for his sin of not respecting rabbinic rules) by staring at him.

The Babylonian text has many additions, and amplifications to this basic framework to explain the sequence of events in a finely crafted and purposely baffling story. This presentation centers on Rabbi Shimon bar Yohai's reputation as a dedicated Torah scholar. Rabbi Shimon bar Yohai was reported, in both Talmuds, to be a fanatic when it came to the issue of the study of the Torah. We are informed that he considered pausing minutes for important things an infringement on his duty to study Torah.[75] Likewise, he argued with Rabbi Yishmael as to the practicality of earning a living when all of one's time had to be spent in Torah study.[76] The version in the Babylonian Talmud has some miraculous elements and, in my opinion, some magical ones as well. Yerushalmi outwardly shows Shimon bar Yohai as a holy man, possessed of the Holy Spirit and able to perform occult acts. The Babylonian Talmud's implied critiques of his intolerance for neglect of Torah study are directly set into the story (likely later additions to the present story) as commentary to highlight the difference between unjustified zeal and justified zeal when rabbinic process is ignored. Just because Rabbi Shimon was imbued with supernatural powers, on its own, is no reason to uphold his views while it is no reason to dismiss them either. Rabbi Shimon's extreme position on Torah study can destroy God's world. The poetry of religious sensitivity, expressed through appreciating God's beautiful creation to celebrate the legal aspects of Torah observance, serves to balance Shimon's extremism. Shimon appears to approve of this approach to religious intuition. Yet the story goes on after this to justify his deed in purifying Tiberias as he did because it met rabbinic approval.

Yerushalmi's version tends to justify Rabbi Shimon's anger towards the *am haAretz*, the Samaritan (the Christian) by presenting a vignette where one of his enemies is indeed a real troublemaker. In the Babylonian Talmud we have the picture of Rabbi Yehudah's comfortable passivity as a foil to Rabbi Shimon's excessive turmoil. In Yerushalmi we have nothing but Shimon's strong reactions. At first glance we are struck by the anomaly to find this story worked into a midrashic message of Jacob's plan to benefit the city of Shechem. But then again the righteous anger of Jacob's sons wiped out the entire city. Before we end with a subtle observation regarding the tensions inherent in the Babylonian version we want to examine the literary traits of the stories.

We note that the Yerushalmi/midrashic story is structured into five units. Each unit can be divided into two parts. The first one contains an initial challenge while the second contains an answer to it. In sections A, D, E Rabbi Shimon miraculously kills off his antagonist. E is the sequel of D. A/D-E provide the frame for BC. Where A begins with Rabbi Shimon casually passing through a place,[77] E ends the same way. But his passing-by brings confrontation and death in its wake. In A the antagonist concurs with Rabbi Shimon's views against rabbinic protocol while in E the adversary had upheld Shimon's opinion in a vote and then rejected it against rabbinic protocol. Yerushalmi has sandwiched the story between two passings where the Rabbi brings disaster to those who reject rabbinic procedures, whether occasioned miraculously or not. In the more original version of the *midrashim* (still preserving tell tale signs of its early oral provenance e.g. "What did he do?") BC stands on one end with sympathy for Rabbi Shimon while D,E,A (so is the order in the *midrashim* B,C,D,E,A) show us a miracle worker full of zeal.

There is a subtle linguistic connection between the sections ofYerushalmi's version showing us a unity of composition: B Shimon hides (tMR) in a cave of TRMH/ They go to Tiberias (tBR) the corpses are made to float up by using lupine beans TRMs. D someone hides (tMR) a corpse. B The world is calm (ShDKh), D they want to cleanse (niDKh) the city, the scoundrel wants to tease (in Pesikta deRAv Kahana: mDHKh; in Yerushalmi: mapli). But also cleansing is reflected in the bird being absolved (DMS), going down to the bathhouses (DMSYN) and the name of the final antagonist NKY (another word for cleansing). The world turns out to be anything but tranquil for him and as he tries to cleanse he ends up taking lives. A unity of sounds and words sews the story into a whole but with confusing reversals. At the end we do not know if it had not been better for Shimon to have stayed in the cave. He is a holy man but his zeal proves deathly for those who reject rabbinic authority. His warning is full of meaning, "The one you buried will rise and live and you will die and descend." Do not trifle with holy men.

6. A FINAL CONSIDERATION OF THE BABYLONIAN READING

What conclusions can we reach about the weight to assign to the Babylonian story? The true genius of the Babylonian Talmud's version is not so much the artful use of *midrashim* that startle us because their origins are so inapplicable to the present situation nor the deep pathos of the tragedy of a simple discussion of three Rabbis. The genius is the introduction of Rabbi Yosi. Rabbi Yosi, known for his tolerance of all valid positions, maintains his silence. We do not know which way is best. Rabbi Yehudah's words gain him honor, Rabbi Shimon's bring him suffering. Rabbi Yosi, who sees both sides as legitimate positions, is banished to Sepphoris where he finds his stature as a venerable sage but he is not banished from the story. The Babylonian Talmud allows us to note the victor could be Rabbi Yosi—whatever you make of the story is the truth.

APPENDIX

RABBI YOSI, THE TOLERANT AND PROGRESSIVE SAGE.

Rabbi Yosi championed the right of individuals over against the established systems. He, teaching in the Galilee just after the bar Kochba wars, fought for the right of the individual to disagree and be heard. When the need arose, as a practical measure, his stance could carry weight and could be cited as a reliable source for sanctioning *de facto* individual rights against the dominating force of prevailing opinions promoting legal consistency. This was certainly true when some leniency had already crept into the system and rabbis needed to find some justification to explain how strict laws had fallen, somehow, by the wayside. His tolerance is cited as a rationalization in the Babylonian Talmud: "according to whose view may we justify that we do X, *ex post facto*? The answer of course is "Rabbi Yosi." He is not seen as any great hero in the tradition for his stances, but his positions on various issues are always stated and the law often follows his opinion. How did the tradition see Rabbi Yosi?

Rabbi Yosi was highly respected. He was born sometime in the aftermath of the Roman destruction of the Temple and rose to prominence in the aftermath of the failed bar Kochba revolt. Historical information is cited in his name and he is thought to be the author of the *Seder Olam*, a work of chronology and midrashic stories. The law often follows his rulings except in some cases where he introduced extreme notions of equity that were inconsistent with the thrust of legal precedent. He seems to have been exiled at the end of life by the Romans if we can trust the above story to have any kernels of hard fact.

Tradition has it that he was one of the Teachers of Rabbi Yehudah the Patriarch, the redactor of the Mishnah. According to the Tosafists he was a superior scholar to the latter. He is mentioned throughout the Mishnah and was one of the most gifted students of the great Rabbi Akiba. Nevertheless, the sages of the Mishnah were not thrilled with his predilection accepting both sides of an argument without the need for further resolution. In short, his espousal of pluralistic attitudes was rather unique but his views are allowed to stand and in times of need even relied upon.

There are only a handful of such cases where Rabbis have justified breaches in the law by recourse to the stated liberalism of Rabbi Yosi. Yet some are worth noting.

In Babylonian Talmud Hagigah end 16a the *baraita* lists one argument concerning a matter of leaning on sacrificial animals on festive days and claims that dispute lasted until the days of Hillel and Shammai. Rabbi Yosi says there really were a lot of arguments but all of them except this one was resolved. This was so because of the court process that had mechanisms for making decisions. He claims that had not this been the case none of these other arguments would have been resolved either. Everyone properly would have continued to maintain the correctness of his individual positions. Individualism is to be cherished and no positions are to be discounted. Further evidence of portraying Yosi's championing individual rights can be found in the Babylonian Talmud, Shabbat 16b. Here the argument is again between Hillel and Shammai. The majority of the Tannaitic Rabbis claimed the argument had been resolved when one side capitulated to the other. Yosi demurred and claimed that the dispute was never resolved. The separate opinions still stand as distinct possibilities with no decision.

Babylonian Talmud Hagigah 22a makes the statement that Rabbi Yosi, above all others, worried about injuring the feelings of others. It cites a *baraita* to show how he asked everyone to treat the purity of wine and oil priestly gifts of the *am haAretz* as if they were totally trustworthy. Otherwise, he argued, they would become alienated to the point of founding their own sects. On this hinge, the much later Rabbi Papa claimed, the custom in Babylonia was to accept the testimony of the ignorant *am haAretz* although technically rabbinic law forbade it.

A further example occurs in Babylonian Talmud Shabbat 87a where Rabbi Yosi claims that although God had wanted Moses to assemble the people to receive the Torah at Sinai on a Friday, Moses, on his own initiative, added a day. Apparently, Rabbi Yosi felt that as long as one can justify one's opinion in acting for the common weal, sages have latitude to so act.

Rabbi Yosi's principle "to enable women to be content" is found only once in the Talmud and then only in passing.[78] Nevertheless, the passage is not mere tokenism. In its application it overrides rabbinic rules of "shvut" (proper behavior on festivals and Sabbaths) and limits the application of "berakhah le-vatalah" (using the name of God in vain). According to the Talmud's conjecture it could allow for the creation of rituals imitating temple sacrificial rituals to avoid cases where such rituals would, if carried out in full form, clearly violate Torah law. The sanctioning of women to participate in religious acts where there are technical problems in Jewish law that would otherwise exclude them, allows us to see the enunciated principle in action: "Kdei la'asot nahat ruah la-nashim (to enable women to be content)." Rabbi Yosi reported hearing from an eyewitness about Second Temple authorities enabling woman to partake in certain ritual activities. Strictly speaking these activities entailed certain technical transgressions. On this report Rabbi Yosi surmised there must have been principles of fairness, which were forgotten about after the destruction of the Temple.

We are not speaking of empowerment or of placating any demands for equality but of Rabbi Yosi's wish to create an environment to give women a sense of spiritual fulfillment even where there are impediments involved in creating the environment. If the nature of the divine law was to forbid women access to ritual the Talmud surmised Rabbi Yosi mandated they perform a "similar ritual" for the sake of giving them religious contentment. That is to say, Rabbi Yosi was sensitive enough to the religious structures of what Rabbis enacted to require that Rabbis be willing to forego "their own systems" to facilitate women to act equally with men, although the ritual was not required of them as it was of men. Furthermore where the Rabbis had no power to allow women to break "a Torah law," they produced rituals which came as close as possible to the male ritual as was permissible by Torah law. The Talmud discusses these possibilities under the rubric of "to enable women to be content. This discussion was taken quite seriously by the Ba'alei ha-Tosafot and subsequently came into Ashkenazic ritual law. The Tosafot argued, amongst other things, that when a woman performed an act that was obligatory for a man but merely optional for a woman the woman could nevertheless pronounce the same blessing as a male would recite. This blessing contains the words "who has commanded us" and women were not commanded to perform positive commandments governed by time. Nevertheless, using the reasoning of the Talmud here, the Ba'alei ha-Tosafot introduced the idea that women could recite the blessings on rituals since these blessings were themselves rituals applicable to the male population and woman themselves were part of the same population of Israel as the males (see Ritva to Kiddushin 31a). Blessings were of rabbinic decree and the Talmud claimed the Rabbis, using the views of Rabbi Yosi, would never interfere with women who chose to follow rabbinic ritual the same as men do. The blessing was separated from the act it blessed as if it became a ritual unto itself. This was an halachic innovation in Jewish Ashkenazic law that was also partially practiced in the Sephardic world as it had the powerful force of a talmudic pericope behind it. There is a fuller discussion in *Siddur Rashi* 267.

The daring of this pronouncement is highlighted in the comments of the Ba'alei ha-Tosafot to Babylonian Talmud Rosh ha-Shannah 33a and to Babylonian Talmud Eruvin 96b. They legislate the ability of women to recite blessings on their performance of commandments they are exempt from. This decision is a total anomaly in the rabbinic legal system.

Yet, even major Spanish schools followed this line of reasoning. We find that the Ritva (to Babylonian Talmud Kiddushin 31a) discusses all the inherent problems and concludes that women indeed can make a blessing on acts they are actually not required to perform. Maimonides, followed by Caro's *Shulchan Aruch*, represents the major opponent of such views. Furthermore, *Trumat ha-Deshen* (by Rabbi Yisrael Isserlein of Austria), *Pesakim u-Ketavim* sec. 132 tells us that Rashi used "Kdei La'asot nahat ruah la-nashim" of Hagigah 16b to permit women, in impure states, (contrary the prevailing custom) to attend synagogue services on the High Holy Days, so they could enjoy the religious atmosphere which permeated the synagogues on those days. Furthermore, Rabbi S. Braun (*Sha'arei Metzuyanim be-Halacha* vol 2, Brooklyn 1991: 425), in dealing with the permissibility to lessen the sanctity of the study hall by extending it for prayer purposes for the specific use of women (who will not study there and consequently the change should be technically impermissible), says "it is a great *mitzvah* to enable women to be religiously content (*la'asot nahat ruah*)" and this principle overrides other considerations of rabbinic law. The addition of Rabbi Yosi to the Rabbi Shimon bar Yohai story is totally in character and acts as a subtle commentary to the entire story.

ENDNOTES

[1]"R. Simeon B. Yohai-- Wonder Worker and Magician, Scholar, Saddiq and Hasid," *Revue des Etudes juives*, 158 (3-4), 1999: pp 349-384.

[2]See pp 352-8: Genesis Rabba 35:2 collected the Jewish Palestinian sources. See pp 361-2: He has prophetic dreams, heals by prayer, exorcises demons (both Babylonian and Palestinian sources).

[3]He lists the miracles in the Palestinian story (p. 365) and in the Babylonian version (p. 366) to clarify the similarities and differences.

[4]His point is that the stories from Tosefta onwards increasingly show him being spiritually elevated as in natural consequence the medieval stories present him as the mystic *par excellence.*

[5]"R. Simeon b. Yohai and the Purification of Tiberias: History and Tradition," *Hebrew Union College Annual 49, 1978: 143-185.*

[6]The third scholar we will engage is Michael Chernick. See below. Another recent work, "The Education of R. Shimon bar Yohai," in Jeffrey L. Rubenstein, *Talmudic Stories: Narrative Art, Composition and Culture* (Baltimore: John Hopkins, 1999: 105-138) has a few good observations amidst a hodgepodge of convoluted findings (e.g. literary/cultural oppositions). In the end he neither explains nor solves the critical issues. Also See Yaffa Binyamini, "The Myth of R. Shimon bar Yohai - A Study in Rabbinic Aggadah," *Mehqere Hag (Holiday Studies): A Journal of Jewish Culture,* VOL 12
2001). (Annual of The Center for Jewish Holiday Studies, Beit Berl College, srael.) Her article appeared too late for inclusion here.

[7]Babylonian Talmud Sanhedrin 98a reports that Rabbi Yosi ben Kisma forecast signs of the coming of the Messiah in terms of the final destruction of Rome. This source reports the day he died the Banyas (Panyas) springs in the Galilee flowed with blood. He also gave a sign reporting that Persia would conquer Palestine. This sign was also reported in the name of Rabbi Shimon bar Yohai in Eicha Rabba 1:41 and Shir haShirim Rabba 8:10.

[8]The words of Yosi ben Kisma come true but the martyr is assured of his place in the Next World. The message is not clear-cut.

[9]"Hanina's Torah: A Case of Verse Production or of Historical Fact? *Approaches to Ancient Judaism*, New Series, vol 1, 1990: 189-204.

[10]"Turn It and Turn It Again: Culture and Talmud Interpretation," *Exemplaria*, 12,1, 2000:63-103.

[11]My few quibbles have more to do with coherence than with lexical definitions.

[12]P. 93 n.57 refers to Alon and Avi-Yonah who saw historical bases to the tales as did Graetz. Chernick seems to discount any historical bases at all to the tales, but see Friedman (below n. 24) p. 132, n. 57. Levine's bibliography (p. 144) is more substantial.

[13]Chernick argues p. 67, 74: Rabbi Shimon bar Yohai has the power even to take life. The implication is that one who studies Torah can aspire to being able to perform amazing feats. I am not enthusiastic about this view because I think the author is embarrassed by the "overkill" and offers the story as a critique rather than an "idolization" of Shimon's Torah study. Rabbi Shimon has not schooled himself under the proper social conditions. Chernick's later words concerning moderation and Torah as contributing to life (p. 76) I find more cogent.

[14]If Maharal (Rabbi Judah Loew) finds the exegesis of Jacob's contribution to Shechem as the basis of what constitutes a civilized city it might be stressed that this view is inherent in the midrash itself. The cumulative aspects are already put together in the voice of Rabbi

Yehudah ben Ilai in Shabbat 33b as well as Avodah Zarah 2b. There need be nothing particularly medieval in this understanding. Scholars sometimes show too much zeal to periodize. If anything, the argument should be the items of baths and money etc. were seen as essential to civilization in early talmudic times.

[15]Chernick (p. 85, p. 92) tells us that Zohar 1:21 7a sees Rabbi Shimon as a mystic who believes in the efficacy of his mystical gem and this is a new development for the Talmud does not know him as such. In fact in our earliest source (Tosefta Kiddushin 5:17) showing Rabbi Shimon's propensity for magic we find him discussing mystical gems. Chernick's view does not hold up. The tales show Rabbi Shimon as a wonderworker. Babylonian Talmud Sanhedrin 98a places Elijah at Shimon's cave in a mystical scene. Also, Babylonian sources create a relationship through marriage with Rabbi Phineas ben Yair, the wonderworker, and Rabbi Shimon. Babylonian sources sometimes like to posit relationships between people of like talents. See further Rosenthal p. 374 and Levine p.179. Cf Babylonian Talmud Ketubot 77b.

[16]So Chernick finds dualities throughout, which are in dialectic tensions of the physical and the spiritual: Carobs (HRB, the root also appearing in sword, destruction) vs Wells (M'YN, the root has to do with eyes, insight); Eden vs. Hell (the cave of the womb and the chamber of hell); Plants vs. Sabbath; Baths vs. Torah; Death vs. Life; Prostitutes vs. Rabbis. All the people Rabbi Shimon encounters are his alter-egos as he struggles with his ideals of super piety and understanding of the human condition.

[17]My impression of the creative reading fills me with the sense that Chernick had hit upon these levels of interpretation because of inner tensions in his personal and professional lives. I heard a similar analysis fifteen years ago from David Hartman of Hebrew University for what I took to be similar personal angst.

[18]Perhaps one might persuasively object that the weight Chernick puts on Elijah referring to Rabbi Shimon simply as "bar Yohai" is unwarranted since Rabbi Yohanan is likewise termed solely as "ben Zacchai" further in the story.

[19]In a few places in the Babylonian Talmud Rabbi Yehudah is given that title. It seems that the sage had the privilege of speaking first in official assemblies and Rabbi Yehudah exercised that right whenever he chose to. Thus Babylonian Talmud Gittin 67a notes that Rabbi Yehudah was the sage whenever he so chose. Chernick (p. 70) gives us "chief spokesman of Jews in all places." I am uncertain if we mean the same thing.

[20]The Mishnah records scores of debates between these three Rabbis.

[21]The implication of Rabbi Yehudah was that Jews derive benefit from Rome's occupation of Judea and Galilee and hence they should acknowledge their appreciation. The ancient custom of the East had been to honor a place when one survived precarious ordeals to arrive at that place. Hence Rome's activities mirrored what earlier patriarchs had done: commerce, transportation, health when camping at hospitable spots. Rabbi Shimon totally rejected seeing the grandeur of Rome as anything Jews should admire.

[22]According to Chernick p. 81 Rashi had motives appropriate to his times for understanding that Yehudah the son of converts (so Rashi takes ben *Gerim*) told his parents the story and in a round about way Rome heard about it. However, it is more likely that he simply is translating the text-- "Yehudah ben Gerim went and related the incident and it was heard by Rome" rather than "fixing the text. If he is doing any fixing" it is because this man was noted to be a sage and particularly caring person in Moed Katan 9a rather than for reasons concerning Jewish-Christian relations in the eleventh century. Such people do not turn in their teachers to the Romans.

[23]One must read into the story in this fashion or the question in part I remains unanswered. The story has been commandeered to answer the question-- or rather the question was posed as an excuse to present the following story.

[24]Yosi's position is not one of fear to speak but a position endorsing the legitimacy of both positions. Some scholars want to correct the text to read "from Sepphoris." (See Friedman's discussion of the issues in S. Y. Friedman, "La'Agadah haHistorit baTalmud haBavli," *Rabbi Saul Lieberman Memorial Volume*, New York, Jerusalem, JTSA, 5753: 131.) According to Josephus, Sepphoris was friendly to Rome and therefore they made it the capital of the Galilee."

[25]Shimon's critical nature is the essence of the story.

[26]According to the Babylonian Talmud, Sanhedrin 98a Yehoshua ben Levi met Elijah standing at the entrance of the cave of Rabbi Shimon bar Yohai. That site is marked in Babylonian talmudic sources as a place of wonders and miracles. It occurs in messianic context In Sanhedrin 98a.

[27]Some emend to read "father-in-law."

[28]While the Babylonian Talmud seems to suggest that Rabbi Shimon bar Yohai knew one of the versions of the later Amoraim which are now cited, it has no idea which version is the original. One notes that the exegesis provided here is responsible for part I of the story "They organize markets. 2. They erect bridges. 3. They build bath houses." This leads one to speculate that another tradition was current in which it was said that Jacob built bridges for Shechem since Shabbat 33b refers to bridges.

[29]After encountering Laban and Esau, his chief enemies.

[30]The word *shalem* has various connotations: welfare, payment, perfection. See Chernick, p.67 for the form by which exegetical materials become interpolated into Rabbinic stories, in my opinion these are not extraneous interpolations but commentary and "foot-notes."

[31]Shama Friedman (S. Y. Friedman, "La'Agadah haHistorit baTalmud haBavli," *Rabbi Saul Lieberman Memorial Volume*, New York, Jerusalem, JTSA, 5753: p. 145) suggests these stories were preserved alongside those of Rabbi Yohanan since the stories share similar motifs and vocabularies.

[32]This parenthetical interpretation of biblical passages occurs as well in the Yerushalmi that knows only the version here ascribed to Shmuel. The commentators speculation the methods of interpretation, some seeing YXN related to "hanut," marketstall, the midrashic versions of the story see YXN "as he got benefit so he gave benefit" reading YHN instead. See Chernick's exposition which is the view upheld by the Soncino translators. I am just following the idea of Pesikta de Rav Kahana here that may be a later view but may not be.

[33]In Yerushalmi the place is identified as Tiberias and Josephus, Antiquities 18:2 ,describes how Herod Antipas built the city of Tiberias on cemeteries circa 18-23 CE creating purity difficulties for the Jewish community.

[34]Presumably he needs to work his magic while situated on undefiled ground; alternatively, we might dismiss the idea of magic here. Perhaps, unlike Yerushalmi, the Babylonian Talmud has a purely rational basis for the cleansing. Knowing that ben Zacchai, the priest, had cut up *trumah* beans here he could assume the area to be purified. The punishment for contaminating *trumah* is very severe. Knowing the area to be pure he could gauge how hard the ground was and anything that hard or harder he would declare pure; anywhere softer he would declare impure.

[35]Levine (p. 166) prefers the reading of the Munich manuscript "ben Azzai" since he is associated with the markets of Tiberias. But ben Zacchai was older than ben Azzai and may

well be the better reading. We think that the place was presumed pure because *trumah* was brought there.

[36]See Yerushalmi Berachot 8:2 for the expression of cutting up *tormosin* beans.

[37]One way to see the matter is that he did that he cut up beans to work some theurgic feat of purification. The word "*trumah*" then becomes problematic." For further examples of rabbinic magic see my "Superstitious Interpretations of Jewish Laws," *Journal for the Study of Judaism* 8 (1977): 127- 38. On the other hand, if Yohanan ben Zacchai did not purify Tiberias but had merely cut up *trumah* in a place he knew to be pure, then the next sentence is problematic. What does "He did likewise" mean? See next note.

[38]The Tosafists, Shabbat 34a think that it means that Rabbi Shimon behaved liked Jacob in Shechem rather than like Rabbi ben Zacchai in Tiberias. Thus he simply used the information that the ground was pure to find a bench-mark for hardness of pure ground. He had nothing to do with beans.

[39]Theodor-Albeck, *Bereishit Rabba* p. 942, cite Palestinian versions where the beans stood their ground where the land was pure but not where it was impure. The sources imply that magic had its effects but rational means were used too. If we follow Rashi's views of the Babylonian sources, Rabbi Shimon did use magic to locate the corpses. We might emend the text and drop the word "trumah." Levine follows this approach and thinks the story means that Tiberias had been partially purified at an earlier time. If this view is taken, both magic and rational means were used. The Tosafists to Shabbat 34a cite Babylonian Talmud Nida 61a whereby wet sheets could be spread over places where it was suspected there were corpses. Where the ground stayed wet it was considered impure and where it was dryer the ground was considered pure. This seems to be related to the features of hard and soft earth. Hard earth held the water on the surface while soft earth allowed it to sink in. Thus the criteria, of how hard and how soft the earth was, would be more obvious by then just touching it.

[40]Whose loose tongue created all the problems in the first place.

[41]This mode of character development is not at odds with that of sections V-VII. The question there was zeal for Torah learning. The issue here is respect for rabbinic, democratic process. I heard from the late Dr. Israel Frankel, a scholar in his own right, friend and mentor, that the expression, "he became a pile of bones," need not mean he died but rather he felt worthless. Sometimes a stern glance from a pious, religious sage can make one feel totally lifeless and ashamed. While I am uncertain this phrase intends this here, I have always thought this interpretation was worthy of the kindly gentleman who proposed it.

[42]Samael is the guardian angel of Rome, Satan. Michael is the guardian angel of Israel.

[43]See RIVASH, Responsa 271 and REMA, Responsa 123, Isserles cites the case of Rabbi Yehudah as a source.

[44]I add an appendix to this piece to show that the position accorded Rabbi Yosi here is consistent with his views as a whole.

[45]All variants of this story in the midrashim and the Babylonian Talmud have Elazar son of Rabbi Shimon featured in the story. The use of plurals in this story also assumes his son is with him.

[46]In all sources except the Yerushalmi, this story comes after Shimon has emerged from the cave. It seems to come first here since it bridges the story of Rabbi Shimon in the cave to another story of Rabbi Shimon that is directly connected with the Mishnah. The story of Rabbi Shimon in the cave is incidental to the first one. However, in the midrashim, the story is the feature because it illustrates a verse and the part of interest to the Mishnah comes at

the end, as a secondary story relating to Shimon's righteous temper. It would seem that the midrash is the original source of the story in the Yerushalmi and that its editor reversed the order of events in the midrash to relate it to the Mishnah.
[47]Compare E: "passing."
[48]In E he asks if the person attacking him did not in fact vote with him.
[49]This is consonant with the Mishnah where Rabbi Shimon Bar Yohai permits all wild growths on 7th year except for cabbage. The Ba'alei haTosafot to Pesahim 51b have another version of this text albeit partially in Babylonian Aramaic where the man is picking cabbage. This version suits the text of a *baraita* that says Rabbi Shimon permitted wild growths of cabbage to be picked on Sabbatical years. "He saw a man picking spontaneous growths of cabbage." The Mishnah says the opposite: he permitted all wild growths except those of cabbage.
[50]Later the story switches to plurals-- "he said let us go down to inspect the baths of Tiberias." Hence I posit the story should be cast in the plural as the midrashic reading of the square brackets suggests. These brackets contain the reading of the midrashic version of Pesikta de Rav Kahana.
[51]Midrash Esther adds: during persecutions (*shmad*).
[52]Looking at Yerushalmi Nedarim 11:1 we find a story about a certain Judah of Uzah (in Babylonian Talmud Nedarim 80b he is said to be Issi bar Yehudah) who did not understand something that Rabbi Yosi had taught. He retired to ponder the question for 3 days. Yerushalmi says he "hid in cave for three days." This source is critical of those who retire from mainstream life, even for a few days, to ponder issues of Torah study.
[53]See Theodor-Albeck Gen R. p. 941 for the reading *harubim* and *temarim*-- carobs and dates rather than carobs of *trumah*. Most likely Levine is right to read "of Gedara" here. The anagram of the Hebrew term *harubin* is RWH BIN-- the spirit of wisdom, while *temarim* can refer to hidden secrets.
[54]That is, covered with sores.
[55]But emerging from the cave proves anything but tranquil for him-- he causes problems.-- apparently the bird story shows he esacped once but not twice. *dimusin*-- he is granted pardon, cleansed, wishes to cleanse himself from the mud,-- wishes to cleanse the city,-- he kills 3 people-- *shadikh, madikh, madikh...*
[56]In Gen R 79 Elazar says to his father that just as the baths of Tiberias have cleansed them, indeed, healed them, so they should cleanse Tiberias.
[57]On reaching Shechem after a period of flight from Esau, Jacob appreciated the city's shelter and offered his talents to benefit its inhabitants.
[58]Chernick p.67 renders: "made butcheries and sold meat cheaply." Levine follows S. Liberman and renders "Duty-free markets" (S. Lieberman, "Ten Words," *Eshkalot-Scolia* III, 1959: 75-81)
[59]Apparently this comment is a parenthetical note, a gloss to explain why he wanted to benefit the city of Tiberias. See Chernick p. 67.
[60]*madchia*
[61]According to Josephus (*Antiquities*, XVIII.2.4) Herod Antipas had built the city over graveyards and created purity problems for its inhabitants.
[62]In Genesis Rabba 79: An Am haAretz came at night, some say from the grain-handlers market, others say from the sack-makers market.
[63]*madchich.*

[64]*temar*.
[65]The one you buried will rise and live and you will die and descend.
[66]In Genesis Rabba 79: *Migdal Zeva'aya.*
[67]Either he did not believe the tradition as in Genesis Rabba ("Yet they say they found a corpse there") or he thought it should not be done by magical means-- apparently the matter had been put to a vote.
[68]In Genesis Rabba: If I do not know of sources as many as the hairs on my head attesting to the purity of Tiberias with a few exceptions.
[69]See Rosenfeld p. 361 for Rabbi Shimon's mystical dreams.
[70]Here we have the rational reason to accept his acts of purification.
[71]In Genesis Rabba. 79 "Concerning the one who breaches a fence, a snake bites him" (Kohelet 10:8).
[72]Levine thinks historically there was serious opposition to the purification of Tiberias. He points out that talmudic sources show Rabbi Shimon as holding very lenient positions in regards to purity issues, Tosefta Ohalot 18:15-18, Yerushalmi Shevi'it 5:1 (Levine p. 170)
[73]To the governors and others of high profile.
[74]For another listing of parallels see Chernick p. 73 and for his list of additions by the Babylonian sources see p. 72. I do not know if all of these are additions or if some things were taken out by the Palestinian sources or even if there were variant Palestinian traditions. Thus, I am confident only about the parallels. I tend to agree that the beginning of the Shabbat 33b version is an addition woven from extant midrashic sources.
[75]See Babylonian Talmud Shabbat 11a.
[76]See Babylonian Talmud Berachot 35b.
[77]And connects with the ruling of Rabbi Shimon in the Mishnah which draws in the rest of the story in its wake.
[78]See Babylonian Talmud, Hagigah 16b.

4

NEW LIGHT IN OLD DARKNESS

HERBERT W. BASSER

I am interested in the history and philosophy of religions.[1] For the past 40 years or so I have had a particular interest in the forms of Judaism that developed over the last 2,500 years. Indeed, I have spent twenty years at Queen's and tonight marks my first public lecture in the University. I hope to be able to communicate at some basic level the sophistication of enquiry that has animated my researches into antique documents written in a variety of languages and jargons over some 8 books and 40 articles. For many, many reasons, it would be inappropriate at Queen's to develop advanced courses in my area of specialization leave alone offer public lectures. I have never managed, for one reason or another, to teach materials related to my research interests here. Several times I have been invited to teach advanced materials in graduate schools at other Universities and eventually, if only once, succeeded in communicating something that changed my life forever. Eight years after I introduced a graduate student (in a course at the University of Toronto) to the journey of the creative impulses implicit in scouting the shores of the books of Jewish mysticism, in a most enchanted moment, we both graduated into that mystical union known as marriage. And our creative impulses have produced two little professorettes who never cease to teach us the mystery of life anew.

My academic interest has been in the classification of the mechanisms of the imagination that has allowed certain writings to hold sway in the formation of particular cultural patterns shared by specific groups of Jews. The classification of these formal rules of imagining an absolute reality or world-view is what I mean by the study of exegesis. Tonight I want to apply some of the things I have learned to a time when two groups whose formal rules of handling the imagination clashed. The collision of world-views gave rise to a battlefield in which the main instruments of inflicting cultural death, the severest form of death possible, were the exegetical tools of mighty warriors. I speak of the battle in which Christianity developed powerful fangs in its oedipal birth throes and rose to menace its parent Judaism.

The chronicles of these battles, the reality of which were often blown up in fictive accounts, would fill many library shelves on the Christian side of the account but much, much less on the Jewish side. Judaism was not defined by its relationship to Christianity, but Christianity was defined by its Jewish context, a context in which it could not survive comfortably and had to shed. The early Christian communities were overwhelmingly populated by gentiles who needed to consign Judaism to the Land of the Dead so as to celebrate the Christian presence eternally in the Land of the Living. We deal with the power of the imagination to make its energies felt in the real, objective world and we deal in a time when Christianity did not yet own the sword of Rome. But its poisoned quills were very sharp.

To dramatize the situation in this time period, at least from the point of view of the 2000-year-old Jew, suppose the person introducing me decided to introduce me as the son of the president of the University. Then suppose I told everyone here that if they did not accept that as a fact all their records, everywhere, would be voided with incompletes and they would not even be allowed to proceed to the parking lot tonight until they accepted that I was Bill Leggett Jr. Moreover they would have to swear to that. In fact, the ushers would announce that the oath was replacing all the institutions of the University. There would be no more classes and no more exams, no professors and no labs. A new era was beginning and everything universities used to offer to their best graduates was now available to everyone without any need even to pass admissions tests. The administrative staff in the University, complaining bitterly, was said to be simply stubborn to deny that Bill Leggett had dissolved everything and authorized his son to usher in the new rule. Those who believed he had done so would get immediate Ph.D's on their way to the parking lot. And to prove their points these believers quoted from the bibles of the University, the course catalogue and the collective agreement. They analyzed particular phrases, atomized them and gave them a shade of meaning that was consonant with what they claimed. The old guard developed imaginative methods of reading these documents to show that the new readings had already been anticipated and discounted. But since the new group had already dismissed the authority of these writings it followed that the new group, even if their exegetical strategies failed might still carry the day. Thus this group risked little in their battles.

This scenario seems to me to be the way Christians were viewed by 99% of Jews two thousand years ago. Jews had no patience for what was clearly nonsense to them and Christians had no tolerance for institutions that were cumbersome and separated out those who had passing grades from and those who did not. The overwhelming majority of Jews would have none of the new claims that promised everything, they thought had to be worked for by obedience to rules, to anyone declaring their faith that Jesus Christ was the son of God. In many ways this Jewish view of Christianity, known as the supersessionist view, was more accurate than not. The general view of Christianity in the period of the Church fathers even to modern times was that those who did the work would never get out the doors and graduate. There is an over-arching parameter for us is to appreciate here; namely, there are places in all cultures where intolerance is a virtue: intolerance of subversive acts, intolerance of perverse teachings, intolerance of national suicide, intolerance of doctrines that undermined the social (read religious) contexts of survival in the light of the physical destruction of the political and religious centers of Judaism. This was so on the one hand. The major structures of Christianity on the other hand suffered from the bloody hand of Rome. But if physical destruction might be bitterly absorbed, cultural destruction could not.

If I have done my work properly both Jews and Christians might well be incensed over what I claim to be a simple fact: Jewish and Christian leaders hated each other before and after the Christian separation from Judaism. Jews may well be embarrassed by my insisting on the vehemence of Jewish expressions of anger and outright hatred, including officially composed curses, against the fledgling Christian religion. Christians, no less may be angered by my claim that the official churches within a decade or so after the spreading of stories that Jesus sanctioned their saints and evangelists to stop at absolutely nothing within reach to delegitimize Judaism and utterly destroy it. Here I will try to document the earliest strata of conflict from the Jewish side; the Christian side is too pervasive to need any new presentation.

In order to put things in perspective, on the Jewish side (which is my overall purpose—since the Christian perspective is easily established and has been for centuries) let me tell you about a case now in the US courts. An American took out a US patent on Mexican yellow beans that he named after his own wife. For every pound of beans anyone in the world sells, this American pirate charges 8 cents US. The Mexicans are angry and refuse to recognize the patent on their own beans. The matter is now before the court. In the same way, first century Christians claimed to have a patent on the very text of the Jewish Bible, its meaning, and the Jewish God. The Jews who had received the text and guarded its every word for centuries were outraged by this act of piracy. There and then began a war which continues in various ways to this very day, for it was in this milieu of strife and discord that Christians put together their foundational documents and thereby preserved this animus as an indispensable part of Christianity. Some may live in denial of it but even so the text has touched them no less as they struggle, in vain, to excuse contemporary Jews from the accusations.

But our issue here cuts more to the bone than a Mexican bean. Every person lives in reference to some culture or other that provides a universe of development for that person. We are not merely bears stuck in a bear world. We live as humans whose essence is composed of the elements of an operating system so sensitive that each particle of it contains the imprint of the whole. Change any key element and the culture is no longer the same culture and the participant of that culture ceases to exist as an intact person. This anthropologically correct understanding of Religion found its breathtaking expression in 13th century

Kabbalistic thought. They spoke of the human being, the Torah, and Divine powers essentially as identities. The human who keeps the Torah performs certain actions mentally and physically which actions strengthen the Divine manifestations. Human beings partake of a sacred cosmos in which they are fashioned through the Torah into mini-divinities that collectively contribute to the divine power that has dictated the Torah. This circle is an objective social reality—a cultural cosmos in which Torah, God and the Jewish people each create each other. In Kabbalistic thought, the number of laws in the Torah correspond to the functions of the body and describe the divine body. Keeping one of the laws strengthens the culture, its God, and its people. Sinning destroys the essence of Torah culture, weakens God's image blemishing his limbs, and creates an unreality or death in the body of the Jewish people. The mythic expression of how culture operates is stunning.

My job now is to introduce you to the concept of the cultural war. In the period I study religion does not exist as a subset of culture. The cultures are religious. Religion is not a part of anything. It is the totality. Today, secular Jews and religious Jews are greatly removed from each other. The religious Jew has no concept of ethnicity, his/her culture is one of thought patterns. His/her behavioral patterns are far removed from the post Enlightenment age the secular Jew lives in. The secular Jew may respect the Hindu, the Muslim, the Christian, even be Buddhist, but he will never respect the ways of the ultra-orthodox Jew; the westernized Jewish presses whether in Israel or outside of it maligns these people.

The religious enthusiasts for the most part know nothing at all of the wider world. But their leaders do and it is indispensable to their culture that they tell stories concerning the depravity of the outside world and instill fear and mistrust of it amongst the growing throngs of adherents to this way of life. The stakes for them are high: their culture, their identity, their values, and their very being.

To make a comparison, although rough to be certain, we can think of the vile rhetoric of the secular camps that look at religious Jews in term of considering them to be the fanatic enemies of modernity and hence of their security in the secular world. The secular Jew, absorbing the disdain of the western Christian world, has long since blamed these Jews for anti-Semitism itself and everything else that plagues Jews. The religious Jews I am speaking about now are stubbornly imbued with a sense of destiny, of love for their culture, living to glorify their identity and pour out their values concretely into a world that wants to destroy their houses of study and their love of commandments. They are hostile to the values of the larger world that mocks the essential contours of their ancestral beliefs passed on for centuries. It is these cultural markers that define their essential being. The canon of Christianity is rooted in the hatred of these beliefs and practices and as such forms a powerful polemic against Torah centered culture and substitutes in its stead a Jesus-salvation centered culture.

Jacob Neusner, in my opinion correctly, writes:

> "The New Testament is an anti-Semitic book, the source of a more formidable contribution than any other piece of writing in all of Western civilization to hatred of the Jews and contempt for Judaism. That anti-Semitism, moreover, is not episodic but endemic, marking not only Paul's dismissal of the "Law" (a.k.a., the Torah) but also Jesus' violent condemnation of the Pharisees in Matthew and Mark, and John's even more hate-filled caricature of "the Jews.".... But the very essence of the New Testament embodies poisonous hatred of "Israel after the flesh," the "Jews," "the Torah" not to mention the dismissal of "Judaism," and all the rest. In the first century the Jews who defined themselves by the written and oral dictates of their culture were threatened by a host of outward enemies. Christianity was amongst the most dangerous threats because it sought to pervert the written and oral dictates and to steal, not the land of the Jews but their peoplehood and their identity. Christian teachers taught that the Jews had been dispossessed of their past and their future.

Christian leaders of later generations would feed off the seeds sewn in these early centuries to cast their biases backwards. In the fantasy of the post-Nicene Church Fathers, Jews who debated Christians always saw the truth at the end, either through persuasion or vision, and converted to Christianity. That was pure fiction, in the first, second and third centuries; wishful thinking, and a literary ploy to convince the Christian reader of the fictive debates of the truth of the Christian cause. Yet, the Church forced Jews to make the fiction into reality in the 13th century. Jews were then forced to debate Christians, the Church judged the debates, proclaimed the Christian side victor, and then on pain of death the Jewish debater was forced to convert to Christianity. Their books were confiscated or burned. The Church Fathers had already provided the super model in fiction, for what later became the fad and fashion of the day. In similar fashion, Paul (Gal 4:22-26) considers Hagar to be the Law of Sinai, the embodiment of the Jews, in slavery for Jerusalem is in slavery, but the spiritual church is free as the heavenly Jerusalem is free. Jews are slaves; Christians are free. It was but a small step for the later church to see here that Sarah, the mistress of Hagar, must be the doctrine of Christ, the embodiment of the Christians who are the masters and the Jews must then be their slaves. In the Book of Genesis, Hagar was the slave of Sarah.

Paul's words were taken to mean that the Jews are enslaved since they are the enemy of humankind. Christians looked through what they took as the eyes of God and saw the Jews to be the perennial other. This meaning is the logical extension of Paul's words, for when Paul wrote the politically weak churches could not have yet enslaved the Jews. His analogy bespeaks the wish waiting for a later fulfillment. When Thomas Aquinas, the great 13th c Dominican ethicist and philosopher of the Church, called the Angelic Doctor, wrote his *magnum opus*, Dominican armies were burning Jewish books and doing worse to the property and persons of the Jews. Aquinas, in his *Summa Theologica* II, 2, 10,10 justifies this activity by subtly referring to Paul's categorization of Jews as slaves of the Church: A Since the Jews are the slaves of the Church, the Church may take disposition of their property (modern translations tone this down). The rhetoric of Paul had led to actual practice in the time of Aquinas.

In the seventeenth and eighteenth century there were Christian Hebraists who wrote about and translated large sections of rabbinic literature into Latin. Their interest , they write , was justified by saying, "While almost everything Jews write is baseless garbage, still out of the sheer quantity there must be something, no matter how tiny, showing some useful insight." In the 19th century Jews began to show that statements of Jesus in the New Testament merely echo the teachings of Pharisees and Rabbis. In the early 20th century a handful of Christian scholars like Herford and Moore wrote very positively about the religion of the Jews but their approaches were put on hold for half a century.

In the meantime the foremost scholars of the New Testament in Germany and even in Scandinavian countries were amongst the very first to pledge allegiance to Hitler and support his anti-Jewish programs. The history of the animosity between the religions goes back to the beginning of Christianity. When it broke away from Judaism, and that break is shrouded in mystery, we know that Jews hated Christians and Christians hated Jews. In fact that hatred was likely deeply rooted before the rupture. That rupture I place in the two decades following the death of Jesus. The hatred and anger was mutual, deep, unrelenting. The most obvious evaluation cannot fail to attract our notice: if Jews are right then Christians are wrong and vice versa; identity and truth were at stake. These are matters that make emotions run high. Without acknowledging this simple fact we cannot hear the texts as they have been read throughout the ages. It is true these texts have proven dangerous but they form the foundational documents of Christianity and cannot be dropped without repudiating the base of Christian doctrine. Ancient and medieval attitudes of the masses are not in any respect so different from those of modern times. Why sully these periods when ours has proven no better at all.

For their part, Jews, greatly distressed by their fortunes turning for the worst as Christianity took over the Roman Empire passed down oral traditions concerning the suspected illegitimacy of Jesus, his tortuous punishments in Hell, or boiling semen to be exact, a list of his crimes and eventually an entire story based on early materials and later embellishments entitled *Toldot Yeshu*, which I take credit for being amongst the first to translate into English.[2] There is of course the danger that Christians reading these materials will find in these tracts the calumnies to persecute Jews more and to consign their writings to the flames. That is why I think these materials were never published in English before this. Did I act responsibly in publishing them? Well the secretary who typed the material quit, and in fact I hesitated for 25 years before publishing the material in a very obscure place. If scholars want to find it they will, but it will hardly make the front pages.

Over the last two decades I read certain texts in highly refined ways to throw light on the antagonisms of the early period. This is no mean feat. The New Testament itself is written in Greek and presents itself as an account of Aramaic dialogues. The parallels I supply are from mainly Hebrew documents of later periods. I am constrained to boil the whole thing down into some kind of elegant presentation in English. My first publication in this area was in 1985 and consisted of verifying certain phrases in disputations appearing in midrashic literature accurately portrayed verbatim citations from Christian Syriac works contemporaneous with the date assigned by the midrash, although the record of this disputation was set down centuries later.[3] Needless to say, to justify my methods would require an entire lecture in its own right and I merely say here that for the casual listener it should suffice to say that the firm evidence of parallels I supply justifies my bold moves.

My approach fills in the large gaps left by such researchers as Claudia Setzer, James Sanders, Alan Segal, Donald Akenson, Mark Hirshman, Steve Wilson, and Geza Vermes and many, many others. Some have missed the mark because they could not accept the deep rooted hatred between the two communities in the first century when Jews and Christians were supposed to be monotheists sharing the same Bible and God and opposing a common enemy in paganism. But it is just this proximity that engendered the mutual hatreds.

In my work, I have not hesitated to substantiate the deep-seated hatred the Jewish leaders expressed towards Christians. They viewed them as a much greater threat than the lure of paganism. While Judaism had no reason to be as cognizant of Christians as Christian had to be of Jews, Christians had to pretend to see Jews as deceivers to justify their anger. But Christians were well aware they had abandoned the entire framework of Judaism (its notion of peoplehood, its dedication to landship, its tenacity in maintaining customs laws and mores) to espouse what Paul claims to be a new framework: promise. In justifying these moves they had to vilify Jews. Jews felt threatened by Christian assertions and successes and took practical measures to keep Christians out of Jewish neighborhoods if possible. As a result there is a huge corpus of Christian materials, many, many volumes, while in Jewish sources there is next to nothing that can be easily identified as anti-Christian. Yet what can be found shows us deep hostility.

In the past I looked at the record of early face-to-face debates between Jews and Christians as evidenced in Jewish writings and found what everyone else had found. The corpus of the Christian materials to amount to thousands of pages; the early Jewish materials would be no more than to fill perhaps two or three pages at most. I therefore set out to uncover references to the great themes of the debates between Jews and Christians in the first century within the most obtuse layers of early Jewish legal works where few if any had looked before.

I considered the history of the development of the New Testament as a book that to my mind fantasized a world in which both Jews and Judaism were supplanted by Christians and Christianity. This fantasy is remarkable for two reasons: first of all, Jews vastly outnumbered Christians in this period. They were thousands of years older, much more established, much better organized in their communities. Christians were not at all hesitant to see themselves as victors over the deeply rooted and established Judaism. I find this to be the first remarkable thing about the early Christian fantasy. The second most remarkable thing about this fantasy is that there is evidence that early rabbinic leaders understood the real threat Christianity posed and took extraordinary steps to counteract it. And of course, most remarkable of all, the fantasy came 50% true and the rest of Jewish/Christian history was the struggle over the other 50%. But that is not my topic. Rather my topic is the search for new light on the Jewish/Christian schism in antiquity. I want to read some texts with you to show you how I think we can uncover a small part of the Jewish side of the debate that has not yet been considered.

Faith Versus Law

Every Semitic religion, whether pagan or monotheistic understood some relationship between the law dictated by the gods and the happiness of mankind. Judaism more than any other formalized the doctrine in promulgating a concept of covenant. Christianity, denied the efficacy of this covenant of the law after the death of Christ and that became the major tenet of Christianity; if the law had an efficacy still then Christ died for nothing. The Jews of course agreed; Yes, that is correct, Christ's death cannot abrogate the law. How did Jews dismiss the claims of Paul? Paul, who styled himself as the "Apostle to the gentiles", strove to prove his points through using the rhetoric of rabbis and Pharisees to deny their own belief system. Let us see take one example and see how the Rabbis dismissed Paul's claim.

Paul is famous for his notion that one is saved from perdition through faith but not through good works. The word for "saved" in Paul's terminology is "justified". There was one early Christian writer, James, who opposed Paul and Luther charged him with being a heretic. Undoubtedly, James' sentiment was a throw-back to the original Jesus cult which quickly lost its hold on the Christianity that developed in the two decades following the death of Jesus. Let us begin by looking at a passage from the OT prophet Isaiah, likely the most oft quoted prophet in Christian literature.

Isaiah 42:21 reads "The Lord is pleased for the sake of his righteousness (*tzidko*); He will magnify the law and make it powerful." This verse is rendered in by the Rabbis in Mishnah *Makkot* 3:16:

"God wanted to justify (*le-zakot*) Israel, therefore he enlarged for them Torah and Commandments. This is as Scripture states: The Lord is pleased for the sake of his righteousness..."(Isaiah 42:21)

The rendition, "God wanted to justify (*le-zakot*) Israel therefore he enlarged for them Torah and Commandments," is meant to be an earnest paraphrase of Isaiah 42:21. Rabbi Obadiah of Bertinoro, in his Mishnah commentary at the end of tractate *Makkot*, affirms the seriousness of this restatement. He remarks that "for the sake of his righteousness (*tzidko*)" (Is. 42:21) literally means to "make Israel righteous (vindicate them); namely to justify them (*le-zakot otan*)," just as the Rabbis in the Mishnah rendered it.[4]

This is the precise paraphrase of *Targum Isaiah* 42:21 (1949): *le-zaka'utei yisra'el; ye-rabei le-avdei oray'tei* ("to justify Israel He increased the workers of His Law"). A variant reading gives us "the works of his law." A Qumran document (4QMMT) refers to "some of the works of the law," and it may simply be that Targum Isaiah utilizes a well-known phrase. However, given the paucity of references to "works of the law" in Targum and rabbinic literature, there is likely more at stake in this reference to "works of the law." At any rate whether one reads "workers" or "works" the intent is to stress commandments of deed.

We observe in these renderings of Isaiah 42:21 a plausible contact with, and refutation of, ideas known from the Pauline epistles and rehearsed many times by Churchmen. Romans 3:28 claims that faith justifies people and not the law at all. A few verses later, Romans 4:2-3, Paul elaborates on this theme by noting Abraham (Genesis 15:6) was said to be justified by faith and *not by works*. Again, Paul says (Galatians 2:10) that man is *not justified by works* but by faith in Jesus Christ. Pursuant to this (Galatians 3:6), Paul refers to Abraham being justified by faith. Paul favors this understanding of Genesis 15:6 since the verse does refer to belief and says it was (reckoned) tantamount to "righteousness;" that is, Paul assumes Genesis 15:6 refers to Abraham's righteousness. Hebrew *TZDK*, righteousness, is usually rendered in LXX and New Testament by forms of Greek *dikaiosis*. The Greek and Hebrew equivalence allows for Paul's observation in Greek that God justifies the heathen, those devoid of commandments, in *faith*. Paul switches the probable referent of righteousness or justification (Targum: *zaku* which mirrors LXX *dikaiosis*) in Genesis 15:6 from God (as some major Jewish commentators do while most do not) to the human Abraham. Now the Septuagint to LXX Isaiah 42:21 understands the referent of righteousness to be God, ("He will be justified") and this is likely Isaiah's intention but the Rabbis have taken the referent to be human Israel ("for the sake of justifying Israel He gave them many laws"). The Mishnaic and Targumic renderings seem fixed at laboring the issue to refute Pauline ideas. Justification is through the law and not by faith alone.

Consider the rabbinic Targum to Isaiah and its restatement in Mishnah *Makkot* in view of Christian contexts. We are struck by the impression that the last two *mishnayot* in *Makkot* (showing that God justifies—*yizkeh lo*—the one who avoids "theft and adultery" and justifies their children until the end of time) address sectarian attacks on the Judaism of the sages. Early Christians were concerned with some ethical laws (yet disregarded most, if not all, ritual laws) of the Bible.

Early Christians specifically mentioned the sins of theft and adultery as Pliny noted in his letter to Trajan concerning Christians.

The ending of Mishnah *Makkot* seems to have borrowed an original, polemical piece of rhetoric once used by sages (in disputations). We see they argued that the ritual laws are easy for people to obey and that by giving the Torah with so many ritual laws (*torah*) and ethical injunctions (*mitzvot*) God was assuring the eternal justification of Israel. The Rabbis stressed that the abundance of Torah laws and prolific commandments are a great blessing. For them it was none other than Isaiah, the beloved prophet of Gospel proof texts, who announces that salvation is through "works of the Law." One exceptional Christian document, as I have previously said, Epistle of James 2:20-24, argued that Abraham (Genesis 15:6) was said to be justified by faith *only* when it was to be established by *actual works*. The justification mentioned in Genesis 15:6 referred to the physical demonstration of faith by the actual works in offering Isaac as a sacrifice in Genesis 22:16-17. Indeed this understanding is also implicit in Jewish commentaries (e.g. Nachmanides), which point to Genesis 15:5 and Genesis 22:17 which say Abraham's reward for faith (Genesis 15:5-6) and his reward in works (Genesis 22:17) is the same reward: his progeny will be as many as the stars of the heavens. Thus the two verses should be combined. James' retort to Pauline ideas of justification through faith rests on solid exegetical grounds. Undoubtedly, Luther was correct in asserting James represents the Jewish side of the debate of justification by faith alone or by faith through physical works. The earliest extant source for an exegesis combining Genesis 15:5-6 and Genesis 22:17 is in 1 Maccabees 2:51. Two centuries before the writing of James, it was recorded that the elderly Mattathias told his sons before he died, "Was not Abraham faithful (Genesis 15:6) *when tested* (Genesis 22:15-18), and it was reckoned unto him for righteousness (Genesis 15:6)?" The complex interpretation necessitating the combining of two verses which share a common theme (progeny as many as the stars) illustrates the antiquity of a form of interpretation the later Rabbis would term "hekesh" or "gezerah shava."

The rabbinic re-statement of Isaiah seems to have migrated from *Makkot* into the current liturgical practice to recite this final mishnah of *Makkot* whenever a mishnah of tractate *Avot* is read in public. Perhaps it was once recited (as in modern times) after public schooling sessions and it migrated into tractate *Makkot* as a natural ending for that section of Mishnah dealing with human and divine punishments. The re-presentation of Isaiah 42:21 shows that the Law, even with its severe sanctions, is a blessing and not a curse. At any rate, its message is a constant reminder to Jews that God loves Israel and that the Law is His instrument to vindicate Israel. If Jews did not refute Christian claims openly with this passage, they certainly said it to themselves in refutation of alien doctrines that disparaged the Law. Complicated exegesis is fine for scholarly debate. To instill conviction, clever exegesis cannot compare to the practical day-to-day intonation of a dogma placed in the mouth of Isaiah, the most messianic of all the prophets of Israel.

I now wish to illustrate, again with a single example, what I have argued in detail in published pieces and various lectures over the years. The discussions between Jesus and the Pharisees that were received in their most original formats were in no way hostile encounters but rather interesting discussions of laws enacted by Sages and rabbis (although the term is somewhat anachronistic in this period). Jesus enlightens his interlocutors as to the mechanisms of rabbinic decrees thus showing limits and boundaries of scribal enactments. Indeed there is nothing in what he says that contravenes ancient, medieval, or modern legal sources. It was the Christian writers at the time of the break with Judaism who cast these discussions into bitter encounters of attack and counter attack according to the debate rhetoric of the times. The animosity expressed in the portrayal of these encounters reflects the anti-Jewish sentiments of the new religion.

A most interesting piece of evidence comes from a work which may be very early although it shows signs of late redaction, *Avot deRabbi Natan.*

Avot deRabbi Nathan A (end of chapter 16) explains the words of Rabbi Joshua: "The evil eye, the evil inclination, and misanthropy expel man from this world" (Mishnah *Avot* 2:11). The matter of misanthropy is explained as follows:

> And what do we learn concerning the condemnation of misanthropy? This teaches that one should not be clever[5] and deduce: "Love the Sages," therefore hate their students,[6] or "Love the students," therefore hate the ignorant; but the proper deduction is "Love everyone" therefore hate the heretics and the apostates [to Christianity] and the informants![7]
>
> And thus David said: "Do I not hate them that hate Thee, O Lord? And do I not loath them that rise up against Thee? I hate them with perfect hatred; I count them my enemies" (Psalm 139, 21-22).[8]
>
> Does it not say, "Love your neighbor as yourself;[9] I am the Lord (*Berativ*, I created him)"[10] (Leviticus 19:18). So then if one behaves as "your people," you must love him, but if he does not so behave, you must not love him.

The latter paragraph poses a question: Does not Leviticus teach us that you are supposed to love everyone, including "heretics, informants and apostates?" This verse is cited to pose an apparent contradiction to the rabbinic teaching encouraging hatred of them and so requires an answer to justify the teaching. As the text now stands, the answer does not respond to the question. "So then if one behaves as your people" does not seem a germane response to the challenge from the love commandment in Leviticus. Something is wrong with the internal logic of the text. To make sense of this, we will have to correct it somewhat. By simply introducing the opening of the verse of Leviticus into the text of the midrash we can comprehend the midrashic passage much more clearly. We suggest citing the biblical verse, Leviticus 19:18, in its entirety and now the end of the midrash will read:

> You shall not take vengeance or bear any hatred[11] against the children of *your people*, but you shall love your neighbor as yourself: I am the Lord." So then if one behaves as "*your people*" you must love him, but if not, you must not love him.

The essence of the homily is clearly being informed by the reference to "your people" in Leviticus. We can prove this by looking at another homily, this time on Exodus 22:27, which says "A ruler amongst your people you shall not curse." Babylonian Talmud *Yevamot* 22b and *Babba Kama* 94b—interpret the ruler amongst "your people" (Exodus 22:27 or some editions 22:28) to mean that one must not curse the ruler; yet, this is so only "if he behaves as your people" (and is not a heretic), if he does not behave that way, then one might well curse him. This latter midrash makes it clear that the Rabbis did not exempt anyone from practicing cordial social norms in respect to those who acted as heretics except in those few cases where Scripture (e.g. Exodus 22:27) explicitly qualified practicing the norm by using the words "your people." Since our midrash, in its extant version, in *Avot deRabbi Natan* qualifies who must be loved and who not by reference to "your people" we must assume the reference is to that part of Leviticus 19:18 which mentions "your people."[12] The midrash has to be emended accordingly. Accordingly, the Rabbis introduced a curse into their prayer service that sought to undermine heretics, some versions explicitly mentioning them, others generically referring to them. It is likely that the context of the above midrash is to be found in the atmosphere of Jewish and Christian disputations of the early Christian Era. The Christians considered Jewish hatred of the Jewish-Christians to be a grave infracture of Scripture that was unjustifiable. Of course, the words of the Sermon on the Mount in Matthew 5:41 are the key to showing the antiquity of these passage. Matthew 5:43-44: "You have heard that it was said, `You shall love your neighbor' (Leviticus 18:19) and [you can conclude] hate your enemy, But I say to you, Love your enemies and pray for those who persecute you." The interpretation of Leviticus did allow for hating Jewish opponents of the Pharisaic sages and the heretical groups opposed to the later sages.

I humbly suggest the following emended version represents the original tradition behind our midrash in *Avot deRabbi Natan A* ch. 16 to read in its entirety as follows.

> And what do we learn concerning[13] the condemnation of misanthropy? This teaches that one should not be clever and deduce: "Love the Sages," therefore hate their students, or "Love

> the students," therefore hate the ignorant; but the proper deduction is "Love everyone" therefore hate the heretics and the apostates [to Christianity] and the informants! Did Scripture not say, "Love your neighbor as yourself, I AM THE LORD"?[14]
> At the opening of the verse, Leviticus 19:18 what does Scripture say?

"And you shall not take vengeance or bear any hatred against the children of your people, but you shall love your neighbor as yourself: I AM THE LORD." So then if one behaves as "your people" you must love him, but if not, you must not love him."

The correctness of this proposed version is enhanced by the realization that it is most likely the scribe's eye jumped from the first citation of "I am the Lord" to the second citation of it and he dropped the intervening lines. The technical term for this jump is homoioteleuton and it is a frequent occurrence in the copying of manuscripts.

At any rate, it seems rather certain that we have here an echo of part of a typical "Jewish Christian versus Pharisee (or Rabbi) debate." In this case the Jewish Christian (real or imagined) opposes the opinion of the Pharisee (Rabbi) that it is permissible for Jews to hate heretics and he cites the biblical verse that stands, first and foremost, as the major principle in Christian thought. The response of the Jewish sage does not minimize the importance of the verse, "Love your neighbor as yourself" (which is likewise a great inclusive principle in the Torah—so says Rabbi Akiva according to the words of the Yerushalmi Talmud *Nedarim* 9:4 and *Sifra to Kedoshim* 19:18). It is not to be underestimated in any way. On the contrary, he says, if it is permitted to hate heretics, despite the major commandment of the God to love all creatures, it must be that God considers sectarians to be the most evil of all and therefore an exception.

Although in some respects Jewish Christians and rabbinic sages shared a common Scripture, it was precisely the mutually antagonistic interpretations of a common canon that engendered so much enmity. In this regard, there is a very important passage in the New Testament Gospel of Luke 10:25-37. It occurs in a passage that is imbued with post-Crucifixion motifs amongst which is the commissioning of missionaries. It appears to be motivated by Church teachings for the community of missionaries. The narrative is broken by a question posed by a Pharisee to Jesus. We know this is a Pharisee because Luke identifies him as a "lawyer" and the term "lawyer" is explicitly used in Matthew 22:34 to identify a "Pharisee" in this variant passage. In Mark 12:28, he is described as a "scribe."

Whereas in Matthew and Mark the issue is not one of confrontation but of inquiry (One asks Jesus, "Which commandment is the first of all?"), in Luke it is Jesus who asks this of a Pharisee who came to test his piety. And in Luke, it is the learned Jew who says, "Hear, O Israel: The Lord our God, the Lord is one; and you shall love the Lord your God with all your heart...(Deuteronomy 6:6) and "[you shall love] your neighbor as yourself (Leviticus 19:18)."[15] Apparently, Jesus asks him to read from a Torah that is conveniently at the scene. Perhaps the Jewish sage brought it for his test. Jesus points out what is written and then asks his opponent to look at two passages "What is written in the Law?" "How do you read?" perhaps an invitation to read the passages aloud. It would seem Jesus points out the responses (namely, "And you shall love the Lord your God with all your heart"..."And [you shall love] your neighbor as yourself") he desires. Jesus then praises the Pharisee for his good answers and tells him if he keeps these two commandments he will have eternal life. Unlike the version of Luke, the versions of Matthew and Mark agree about the interchange in so far as it is Jesus who tells the Pharisee the two love commandments without asking leading questions. All in all, Luke seems to have modified the original interchange into a forum in which the Pharisee appears to have been bested on his own reading of the Law.

To continue with the Lucan passage we find that the lawyer continues the debate in order to justify his rejection of Jesus, "And who is my neighbor?" he asks. The answer, again elicited from the mouth of the Pharisee, is somewhat unexpected: a merciful Samaritan (a sectarian whom one might categorize as heretic and enemy) might be a good neighbor if he shows compassion.

This question "and who is my neighbor" forms the pivot of several Jewish/ Christian debates in both Jewish and Christian sources, not necessarily because Jews excluded non-Jews from this commandment; Leviticus 19:33 itself forbids the exclusion of converts and resident aliens. Yet, the Rabbis excluded heretics and apostates; namely, Jewish Christians.[16] This exclusion was the source of friction between Jews and Christians in the early rabbinic period and perhaps the Gospels contain some evidence of the Jewish exclusion of Christians from the love commandment in the first century.[17]

Rabbinic sources have several references to the problems caused by Christians using Israel's Scriptures and even seeing themselves as the Israel mentioned in them.[18] Several of the Rabbis held Jewish Christians in contempt for this very reason alone. One of them is reported to have said if someone were to chase after him to kill him, or even if a snake were to pursue him to bite him he should take shelter in an idolatrous temple rather than run into a Jewish Christian church. The reason given for this advice turns out to be that the latter are worse than idolaters are since they know the divine will and deny it.[19] The Rabbinic sources hint of heated debates between the two sides in antiquity. While we have hundreds of documents specifying the Christian views of these debates we really have next to nothing on the Jewish side of things until the Middle Ages. And it is here that most scholars of polemics begin their inquiry for it is here that old lights shine. The earlier materials, even when exposed to new light, remain fuzzy and that is the reason I think they are more interesting.

ENDNOTES

[1]Lecture given for Jewish Studies Series, September 2000 at Queen's University.
[2]"The Acts of Jesus," *Frank Talmage Memorial Volume*, Part I, Haifa University Press, 1993: 274-282.
[3]"The Meaning of 'shtuth,' Gen. R. 11 in reference to Mt. V:29:30," *New Testament Studies* 31 (1985): 148-151.
[4]Professor James Kugel of Harvard University has told me in private communication he considers this "midrash" to be a style of translation into rabbinic Hebrew.
[5]Probably one could argue that the commandment, "And you shall love your neighbor as yourself" refers to that neighbor who is "as yourself"—a sage (to sage), a student (to a student), an ignoramus (to an ignoramus) depending on who you are yourself.
[6]This is not a proper deduction of what is discouraged by the term "misanthropy." The opposite would be "philanthropy"— love of one's fellow. Who is included as "one's fellow" forms the context of the teaching. Apparently, someone is to be excluded but it is difficult to know why this assumption is made. All we can surmise is that the tradition of "love of neighbor" precludes any hatred. Why then does it not preclude hatred of apostates?
[7]Schechter's version of *Avot deRabbi Nathan* 64. Compare the list of enemies of the Rabbis in Tosefta *Sanhedrin* 13:5.
[8]His passage is a late scribal interpolation in the pericopae. It is found in Babylonian Talmud *Shabbat* 116a, Jerusalem Talmud *Shabbat* 16:1, *Semahot* 2, Tosefta *Shabbat* 14:4, *Mekhilta of Rabbi Ishmael Beshalah Shirtah* 6, *Sifre Deuteronomy* piska 331. The passage cannot be integral to the midrash as it renders the remainder of our midrash as redundant in that it provides a biblical verse to justify hating heretics. That is the whole point of the remainder of the pericopae. The passage should be bracketed as an addition.
[9]We just finished saying that the intent of these words is not to exclude anyone—how then can you now make exclusions? Some texts add "And why is that?" here.
[10]This is not part of a biblical verse nor is it a known midrash, but an error that made its way into this text, and into the next text: "Love your neighbor as yourself, I am the Lord, I created him." Goldin (in his translation 1974) renders here: "Because I [the Lord] have created him." He appeals to Isaiah 45:8 which he thinks accounts for the reading here. This is indeed how the text reads but it is highly dubious this reading is original. It adds nothing relevant to the point here nor to the point of the next passage. It seems to have made its way in here by a scribal error of some late copyist. Undoubtedly, it belonged to another midrash, now lost, which provided the rational for adding the words "I am the Lord" after "And you shall love your neighbor as yourself: God created both him and you." I suspect there had once been a collection of "Love your neighbor" midrashim.
[11]This is rendition in both the Jewish *Targum Onkelos* and the Christian Syriac translation of the Bible or *Peshita*.
[12]For a paraphrase of Leviticus 19:18 in this regard see *Avot deRabbi Natan B* ch. 26: If you love your neighbor whose behavior is proper in the way yours is, then I the Lord am certain to have mercy upon you. That is the verse is read by equating the phrase as yourself in "love your neighbor as yourself" with "children of your people", that is, if you act as a proper Jew and someone else does not then it is proper not to love him. But if you do not act properly and he does not act properly and you hate him then God will punish you, and if you act properly and he acts properly and you love him, then God will love you. That is why the verse ends with the notice: I am the Lord.

[13]Hebrew "keitsad": the term is used in Tannaitic literature of the two first Christian centuries as a way of asking what further details we have concerning material known from more general teachings of Rabbis. We should therefore date this material to the earlier strata of debates.

[14]Exclaims the Christian or the author anticipating what such an opponent would retort.

[15]This passage cannot be used to justify the claim that Jews juxtaposed the two love commandments in the first century. Matthew and Mark have the juxtaposition in Jesus' mouth and this seems to be the original tradition. Luke has cast the scene in typical debate form that requires the opponent be led to affirm Jesus' position and is therefore put into the mouth of the Jew. Luke apparently changed the focus of the teaching from Jesus to the lawyer to create a debate in which Jesus would elicit his teachings from the mouth of his opponents. Rather than see here an original Pharisaic teaching, it is more likely we have an undermining of the Jewish exclusion of heretics and Christians from the term "neighbor" in Leviticus 19:18. Luke's scene need not be understood to mean that first century Pharisees had juxtaposed the two love commandments in the way Matthew and Mark present the teaching.

[16]While Luke could not really speak of Christians in his Gospel, there were none in the time of Jesus, he could speak of another fringe group considered as heretics by the Scribes. Hence he utilized the figure of a Samaritan.

[17]According to the *baraita* in *Kallah Rabbati* ch. 6 when Rabbi Eliezer was on his death bed he told his students that they should be careful about the honor due one's fellow and to have full awareness of their devotion to God when they stand in prayer. The talmudic commentary in this minor tractate refers to "And you shall love your neighbor as yourself, I am the lord." But does not cite "And you shall love the Lord your God." There is no evidence here that Jews juxtaposed the two commandments although love of mankind and love of God were recurrent themes in their sermons.

[18]See *Tanhuma* "ki tissa" beginning of 34. [The Gentiles say:] "And we are Israel." The Christian view is put forward by Justin Martyr in his *Dialogue with Trypho.*

[19]See Babylonian Talmud *Shabbat* 116b.

5

MAKING EMENDS: MAINTAINING A CULTURE

REENA BASSER, QUEEN'S UNIVERSITY

1. INTRODUCTION

In this essay I want to deal with a feature that is familiar to those of us who study the history of the interpretation of authoritative debates and teachings assembled by the Jewish sages 70-530 CE. This history shows us the assertive attempts of sages to harmonize, reconstruct, and emend impenetrable statements in the tradition.[1] Not only did the text have to make sense, it had to conform to other teachings current in the community that were understood to be already conforming to canonized authority. Quite often there were tensions between what texts in fact said and what teachers taught. The study of the mechanisms through which such problems were confronted has never been undertaken in any systematic way. It is my task here to outline, but by no means exhaust, the strategies of the ancient sages as they dealt with these particular issues and to illustrate how these strategies continue to operate in Jewish teachings until the present day.

Attention to wording and context is indispensable for the modern student of these texts. Professor Neusner has supported the publication of some five or six volumes of critical editions (or synoptic editions) and in his own work is careful to consult critical editions based on examinations of manuscripts. His visit to Queen's, November 26, 2001, adds stature to our fledgling program and his support for our programs has been legion. Not long ago, he offered to stock the library with his studies, free of charge. However, the library discovered they would have had to build a special wing to make room for the hundreds of volumes and they had to decline his generous offer.

2. The Issue

Professor Daniel B. Sinclair has detailed the salient features of an exchange between the foremost *halakhic* authorities of the twentieth century, Rabbis Moshe Feinstein and Eliezer Waldenberg.[2] Rabbi Feinstein presented his decision but found that both the Ba'alei haTosafot and Rabbi Yosef Trani, contradicted a view he held to be the unanimous opinion of the *halakhah*. He was forced to say that the wording of the *Tosafists* had to be a corrupt printer's error and he emended it in accordance with his view. He then proceeded to proclaim the second half of a *responsum* by Rabbi Yosef Trani to be a forgery. After these moves, there could be no objection to his stringent point of view. Rabbi Waldenberg remarked that this was not a proper way to pronounce *halakhah* and no decisor in the entire history of Jewish legal process had ever used purely conjectured sources to prove a point. Undoubtedly Rabbi Feinstien, the master of legal decisions of this century, instinctively knew how the legal tradition had to eventuate in regards to the matter before him and if certain texts stood in his way, all the worse for the direction of those texts. Indeed, we might find warrant for Rabbi Feinstein's attitude should we examine the methods used by earlier sources.

3. A Short History of Emendations of Mishnah by Babylonian Rabbis

The Mishnah is a work that marks the close of the period of the Tannaim. These were scholars who sought out, sorted, selected, and debated various rules and regulations concerning every facet of Jewish life. These scholars also showed how these numerous rules and regulations derived from the Holy Scriptures. When a Scriptural passage conflicted with some current oral teaching or cultural norm a vast array of hermeneutical devices was available to help solve the conflict. One such rule was termed "If it is unnecessary for Scripture to have stated this case because we already know it, let us apply the rule to a case we do not already know."[3] The antiquity of such a hermeneutic is already apparent in a biblical exegesis preserved in the Gospel of Matthew. The point under discussion is that Leviticus 19:18 is too obvious. "Love thy neighbor as thyself," cannot simply mean to love your fellow Jews who are your friends and not care about your enemies. Why would the Torah have to tell one the obvious? Although this is the manifest sense, surely the Torah has to be talking about a case that is not so obvious. It must somehow refer to a case where we have to love our enemies.

Matthew 5:46-48:

> For if you love those who love you, what reward have you? Do not even the tax collectors do the same? And if you salute only your brethren, what more are you doing than others? Do not even the Gentiles do the same?

> You, therefore, must be perfect, as your heavenly Father is perfect. (And he makes the rain to fall and the sun to shine on sinners and righteous alike, Mt 5:43-45.)

The New Testament concludes that Leviticus is dictating that one should love one's enemies. This sermon is not as some have surmised a reversal of Biblical teaching but rather an application of a complex hermeneutical rule for dealing with Scriptures that do not agree with the wider teachings of the preacher's ideals. The Leviticus text has not been emended but it has been rerouted to shed light on a teaching that is not at all its simple meaning. Tannaim used this method at times to serve the needs of biblical interpretations when the obvious sense was accepted but another teaching implicitly developed as if it was the intended teaching of Scripture.

This idea that Scripture would not waste precious words on the obvious became transferred to Mishnah interpretation. Many times over the Babylonian Talmud complains about the Mishnah, "Too obvious!"[4] It proceeds to apply the wording of the Mishnah to a case that is not at all obvious. On about five occasions of the hundreds, when this strategy was used and the new application would seem too far-fetched to be derivable from the wording of the Mishnah, the Talmudic Rabbis emended the wording of the Mishnah to arrive at the needed results. That strong measure was a sign of the pressure the Talmudic teachers, *circa* 300 CE and later, were under to get earlier teachings to conform to their general system.

But the teachers of traditions in the second century already found ways to re-apply teachings that were not consonant with wider concerns of the legal system. They would teach what they had received and then they would add: "To cover what narrow circumstance was this taught?"[5] The improbable case would be given followed by a restatement of the law as it was to be generally observed. This strategy of qualifying teachings to apply to very limited circumstances allowed the teacher to state the rule to apply to the general cases which was consistent with pressing concerns. Our sources show us the unqualified teaching in one document and qualified in another.

At times, when push came to shove, later teachers emended some tannaitic traditions by claiming there had been qualifications already in effect but the received texts were defective and had inadvertently dropped them in the process of transmission. Or else, when the later Amoraim wanted to deal with statements of their own Amoraic teachers, statements which were in discord with other matters, the later teachers would likewise restrict some of these teachings to narrow cases. They would restate the larger matters in conformity with adhering to the authoritative pronouncements that held sway. In either case, their formula would be to cite the teacher and remark, "Here, with what particular case are we concerned?"[6] Then by claiming that only a single case was intended, they were free to restate matters consonant with other current teachings that had developed, perhaps before the

Mishnah had ever arrived in Babylonia. In all cases the authority of the Mishnah and its original teachers was maintained, even if its application was greatly restricted and other laws were practiced that had their origin in non-mishanic traditions. But the tendency to reduce hard sayings to minimum cases had already begun prior to the production of the Mishnah and sometimes such restrictions appear in Mishnah itself.

The process of emendation, according to reports, began as soon as the Mishnah was brought to Babylonia. The Talmud (Eruvin 14a) reports that the first Amora, Rav, could not accept the received wording of a mishnaic passage as it stood. He instructed his children's tutor, "Teach my son this emended version, etc., etc." Rabbenu Tam, in his comments to the Talmud, claims our received texts of Mishnah actually reflect Rav's proposed change rather than the original wording of the Mishnah. Rabbenu Tam argued that the Mishnah was reworded because the *halakhah* was like Rav in this instance. Tosafot ha-Rosh is amazed at this development because, even though the law is often like Amoraic emendations to the Mishnah, the received wording of the Mishnah never seems to have been changed in a single case. There is little warrant to suppose it has been changed here. The most common expressions used by the Babylonian Talmud to state that one is forced to restate matters through emending the text are: "Say it this way instead,"[7] "Let us supply some words and phrases which are missing ,"[8] "subtract this and add this,"[9] and "Change the words (names, cases) around".[10] We find that there is room for innovation while still adhering to the words of the tradition.[11]

The Babylonian Talmud often emends questions or statements of teachers in some quasi way because it cannot find any meaningful context for them without doing so. These quasi emendations, conceptual doctoring, are sometimes introduced by such phrases as: *hachi mibai leih* ('this is what it should have said"), and *hakhi ka'amar (katanei)* ("this is what it meant to say"). What we witness in these cases is an attempt to redefine matters without actually doing much violence to the received wording. The innovative meaning assigned to the teachings strains the text. The reasoning is impeccable; the only trouble is that the words do not say anything of the kind. License to manipulate text is a strong feature of the Babylonian Talmud. The impression one gains from dealing with these matters is that the devices used to circumvent the literal sense of the Mishnah were employed with total sincerity. The scholar responsible for the change appears to have really believed he was accurately reconstructing the tradition. It was sufficient and necessary to use these tools. Maimonides, in his Introduction to his commentary to *seder zera'im* of the Mishnah notes that the redactor of the Babylonian Talmud did what was patently humanly impossible by formulating the precise and definitive meaning of the Mishnah through accepting a host of techniques including emendation. No one has the right after the closure of the Talmud to use these methods to change anything at all. People can only study Talmud and understand, not innovate. The reconstructed tradition is total, perfect and decisive.

Having noted that pronouncement, we must also note that the wordings of the textual traditions behind the Talmud were in flux and different schools had different versions. The Talmud sometimes remarks about mishnaic readings: "The one who transmits this word with an *aleph* (with one meaning) is not in error and the one who reads this word with an *ayin* (with another meaning) is also not in error."[12] The reason they are not in error is because both readings are equally possible, although undoubtedly only one is original to the Mishnah. What is defensible is acceptable.

The Talmud often refers to different versions of a text, sometimes by noting there was a divergent tradition: "Here is how some people said it and here is how other people said it." Sometimes the Talmud cannot reconcile conflicting opinions reported of the same teacher. So the Talmud assumes that two students or professional reciters passed down opposite traditions of what the master had said.[13] The Talmud often changes matters by saying: "If was taught at all, it must have been taught this way."[14] The passages continue with emendations of what was originally reported and the Talmud substantially alters the reported words to accommodate whatever issue has to be accommodated. Another method to dismiss specific matters is to claim that such matters were never actually said by the teacher who was reported to have said it. Rather that teacher had established certain principles and someone else on the basis of these principles surmised that the teacher surely could have maintained such a teaching.[15] The net effect was as if he said it since he implied it. Then the Talmud shows the teacher could not possibly have held that implied position and dismisses the whole teaching as erroneous.

What we note here is the reconstruction of the authoritative tradition to fit some total scheme of matters. It might well be that the scheme fits the earlier, pre-mishnaic teachings that were currently practiced or some philosophic notion of the way matters ought to proceed. We cannot know the motives for certain. Yet, we are constrained to admit that what looks to us like willful meddling and doctoring was really a sincere attempt to establish a coherent system of talmudic law. On the other hand drawing implications from texts, both biblical and mishnaic, and attributing them to the very texts themselves is a commonplace in rabbinic literature.[16] An interesting example is Babylonian Talmud Yevamot 25b. Rabbi Ashi derives a teaching from the Mishnah and says his law is a Mishnah although no one else had any inkling of his source. The strategy of the Talmud to discount matters by suggesting that later Amoraim had made a problematic inference about what their teachers said is certainly plausible.

4. The Manner of Treatment of Reconstructed Tradition.

Invariably forced interpretations or emendations become codified as standard *halakhah*. The reason for following these forced readings or explanations is as follows. The Talmud goes to the lengths of introducing forced modes of emendation or interpretation to justify a particular *halakhah*. It must be the case that the Talmud was forced to act the way it did because the practice that was in vogue could not be justified by recourse to any authoritative text unless that text was somehow altered or forced to mean something apart from its plain sense. The Babylonian Talmudic voice wanted these particular concepts to be operative and pushed matters to yield these meanings. The Yerushalmi is much more conservative and does not, it seems, willfully emend.

5. History of Medieval Emendation of Talmudic Texts

We find that Maimonides also went against the common decisions of his predecessors and emended Talmudic readings but he did so only after he located the reading he wanted in a real manuscript. Thus, in the 15th chapter (*hal.* 2) of the *Laws of Loans* , in his *Mishneh Torah*, he tells us he consulted all the readings of a passage and finally found what he was looking for in a parchment text of the Talmud he had purchased in Egypt and that Talmud was close to 500 years old. Rashi (Arachin 12b) also remarks that he had wanted to emend a text based on his own logic and understanding of matters but that his teachers objected until he actually located an ancient, precise manuscript with the very reading he had conjectured. Then, and only then, did his teachers accept his emendation of their texts. Rashi refers a few times to the readings in the Talmud owned by Rabbenu Gershom (Sukkah 40a). Nevertheless, Rashi suggested many, many emendations to the Talmudic text (my data-base search records over 2300 times) most often based on his own ideas of how things should flow. Rabbenu Tam (See Introduction to *Sepher haYashar*, Berlin 1898) objected that Rashi's students had changed the wording of Talmudic texts to accord with Rashi's conjectures although Rashi himself simply noted his conjectures in his commentaries. Apparently, the older medieval commentators were reluctant to change received readings without hard evidence to do so. Mere conjecture was insufficient. The text was always the received text; the reading of the text was another matter. The late Professor Shlomo Morag tape-recorded the Talmudic readings of the Yemenites and noted in many cases words might be written but the student read them as something entirely different. Thus, the integrity of the received text was maintained and the necessary logic to maintain the text was provided for.

In the West, it was the stature of Rashi that brought about the change in attitude towards conjectured readings. Rabbi Joseph Caro, *Shulchan Aruch* 279:1, tells us that conjectured changes must never be written in a text but only recorded in marginal glosses for perhaps someone will come someday to defend the problematic reading. And indeed anyone who studies even one page of Talmud today will likely find glosses suggesting emendations to the Talmudic text. Ritva often reacted against the tendency to change texts by recording conjectured emendations and then noting the readings of older manuscripts. More problematic is the case where we find Talmudic readings of biblical verses that are not to be found in our versions. Whereas Rashi and Rabbenu Hannanel are content to simply cite the Talmud's biblical verses in the way they appear in the manuscripts, *Ba'alei ha-Tosafot*, followed by many early commentators and almost all later commentators, would drop the sentences in the Talmud dealing with the slippery verse and erase them from their texts in marginal glosses. They saw the suspect verses as grossly corrupted by scribes. For example, could the Bible really say, ask the Tosafists (Berachot 61a), that Elkanah, hardly a boor or *am-haretz*, really walked behind Hannah his wife![17] Surely such a text never existed and it is certainly not found in our Bibles.

After the time of Rashi, early commentators were fond of producing creative readings when all else failed. That is not to say they did not consult other manuscripts. They surely did and often told us to look at the wordings in the Yerushalmi and *midreshei halakhah*. *Rashi and the Ba'alei haTosafot* prefer to cite variant readings they find in earlier sources, including Geonic works such as *Halakhot Gedolot*. And other times they emended *midreshei halakhah* according to the text of the Babylonian Talmud if that text made more sense to them and vice versa. Nevertheless, at the end of the day, they all accepted their texts had to be corrupt in many, many places.

The commentators believed, with good reason, that a plethora of corrupt readings had entered the texts in the course of its lengthy transmission. They suggested emendations based on their own tight reasoning but also based on what they thought were variant citations of Talmud submerged in the paraphrases of early authorities like Rabbenu Hannanel. In short, whatever reasons could be found to judge between readings or to produce new ones, these reasons were always based on the sense of the internal logic of passage as perceived by the reader.

6. Justifying the Practice of Emendation and Re-interpretation

Concerning more recent times, we note that the Vilna Talmud lists the emendations of *Gra, Bach, Maharsha, Reshash*, and scholars who would alter Talmudic texts. On what authority do they do so? The authority to reconstruct a text is the authority of human reason preferably aided by hard evidence. Texts may be changed because they run counter to the accepted tradition and may therefore seem corrupt. This may not seem to warrant changing a reading attested in all witnesses but the change is necessitated in light of the larger tradition. The change of gross error is a simple matter and such changes need no other warrant. It need not concern us to change the confused masculine forms of ten to feminine forms when the Talmud records the measurements of *amot*, a feminine noun. We can do that easily. It is apparent to anyone who has studied manuscripts that intuitive correction is a hard and fast feature of reading Hebrew manuscripts. It is true that Jewish law requires that uncorrected texts cannot remain in their corrupt state for over 30 days.[18] Nevertheless, the widespread sloppiness of scribes was often left in most manuscripts undoubtedly because the owner of the manuscript had no problem mentally correcting the text where there were gross errors. More subtle errors still plague us whether by copyists or by printers. Nor has the computer age really helped us be more accurate as computers can generate their own types of errors that are very difficult to catch.

J.N. Epstein, the eminent scholar of Talmud, distinguished between variants and versions in text types. One might think this distinction could hold true for texts, which were orally taught and transmitted, but could not hold true for texts that were written originally. However, we find that written texts also come in versions, and we are forced to think that perhaps authors or students reviewed their own works or their teachers' works over time and thus produced different versions. It is simply quite astounding how common different versions are. The Yerushalmi and *Heikhalot* readings, generated by P. Schaefer in his synoptic editions, are but a single case. Even if it is true that many of his versions will turn out in the end to be simply containing variants, there are still multiple versions to be found of these texts.[19]

We sometimes confuse versions with variants. We can note how the Ba'alei haTosafot once in a while corrupted their perfectly fine readings of the Talmud which was brought to Germany and France, through routes altogether different from that of the Spanish tradition. Perhaps one text was edited in Sura, the other in Pumbeditha. Or, perhaps one version was adjusted by Saboraim (Talmudic editors) and the other was not. The importation of Eastern texts in Northern Europe through copying the commentary of Rabbenu Hannanel of Kairowan, or from the Yerushalmi tradition known to the early medieval commentators, or from *midreshei halakha*, coupled with the boldness to emend texts by *divinatio* resulted in the German-French text becoming a hybrid text. After the time of the Ramban (1300 CE), these texts reached Spain and became part of the tradition there. Ritva, a short while later, sometimes lines up many different versions in order to establish which was the original Spanish reading.

7. Modern Approaches to Textual Editing

Let me now distinguish between, gross error, variant, and version and pretend that the fuzzy lines between them are in theory quite sharp. A gross error often is caused by a scribe becoming distracted and copying nonsense, perhaps skipping some words, perhaps recopying a line he has already copied, or perhaps just misreading the words. These are many humorous cases of such errors, like the scribe of Esther who wrote *ishti*, my wife, when he should have been writing *Vashti*, the rebellious wife of King Ahasueros. A variant is noted when we compare two texts both of which say the same thing but in slightly different words. It may be that way back in the early copying of the text a scribe glossed a difficult word with a simpler synonym and included both words. A later scribe perhaps just chose to copy the easier word. We might now have three texts of which each one really means the same as the rest except a synonym occurs in some of the manuscripts. Moreover, some occurrences are frequent in texts that were transmitted orally before being recorded. They are true variants in which both versions are equally original to the written tradition. At some point we have to make a decision which word, if any, is more original and which the variant. In most cases, corrupt variants occur when a scribe misreads a word, with a plausible sense, or a student mishears a word or repeats what he has heard imprecisely. In these cases we have to study our manuscript families and try to judge which families are most distant geographically but closest textually.

In general, we may posit that if two manuscripts agree on a reading, where others differ, and these two come from different ends of the world (so it was unlikely that scribe A knew the manuscript tradition of scribe B) we can assume the agreement of A and B indicates we have here the original reading. It is a fact that scribes corrected one manuscript against others that he or she could find, so agreements caused by contamination mean nothing to us. If we can rule out cross contamination of readings we can locate original citations. There is reason to think that medieval scribes sometimes adjusted texts before them according to the readings they were most familiar with and what made best sense to them. Often commentators quote texts in forms compatible with their own understandings by omitting or adding what they would. Given this fluid state of affairs I cannot help but advocate that the modern text editor be granted the same privileges. When one restores lost art and has no idea of what the original was like, he must study the painting and surmise what makes sense. It is either that or he leaves matters as they stand without any attempt at correction. I opt for the first method providing that the corrections be indicated somehow except for obvious gross errors that may be safely emended without as much as hint of what barbarism actually was in the text.

Rabbinovicz attempted to produce an edition of most of the Talmud based on the fuller text of the Babylonian Talmud which is evident in the Munich manuscript, the only complete manuscript in our possession albeit in photographs.[20] Other partial manuscripts have been photographed and published. The current projects of producing critical editions of Talmud which cite the variants found in other manuscripts and commentators goes a long way towards clarifying the text. Critical editions of various tractates have appeared. Still, translators and scholars favor the received text of the Vilna edition of the Babylonian Talmud as evidenced in its reconstructed readings placed within square brackets. That is because this text closely accords with the version hypothesized by Rashi.

8. Conclusion

Let us look more closely at the apparently cavalier attitude of rabbis of all periods towards the integrity of the texts. We find that the talmudic sages plausibly determined that there were tell-tale signs of scribal emendations in the Tanak—

whether they meant by God or by someone else is still a matter of debate.[21] These emendations were said to be protective of God's honor and certain widespread Near Eastern scribal customs were observed in the copying of the Tanak. As well, we find that there was a rabbinic tradition of scriptural emendation that reportedly had occurred in the time of the Second Temple, based on the comparison of two out of three Torah scrolls.[22] In the Talmudic period we find the Mishnah was subject to emendation in order to understand the text and according to some scholars changes were incorporated into the very recitation of the text of the authoritative Mishnah. In all subsequent periods we find that scribes introduced variants and corrected texts, sometimes according to reliable textual witnesses, sometimes forced by the need to produce an intelligible text. Ideally, each version of the whole Talmud was subject to its own history of transmission and the reworking of its own set of variants. However, the idea of a version as distinct from a variant was little appreciated and quite often one version became contaminated by reference to variants in another version. Thus we can applaud attempts in all periods to refine the wording of manuscripts based on ideas of cleaning texts from interpolations, copyist errors and acceptable polite conventions.

But we should not lose sight of the most common reason for emendation; namely, to bring the system together into unified legal and theological understandings. Let us look at the kind of reasoning attributed by the sages to Moses. On three occasions, they tell us, he rethought the directives given him by God.[23] First, he decided to divorce his wife. Second, he brazenly decided he would smash the tablets of the commandments. Last, he decided to receive the Torah on Shabbat rather than on Friday as God had seemingly told him. The Talmud says he did these things of his own accord and then gives us his methods of textual reasoning to justify his actions. Tosafot is correct to point out that if he used textual reasoning he did not decide these matters of his own accord.[24] These Tosafists point out that Moses had his own reasons for changing matters as they stood and the textual reasoning was somewhat superficial, not iron clad exegesis at all. It looked possible that what Moses did might have had some warrant but in fact there was very weak warrant. Nevertheless, God agreed with his decisions. In so doing the Tosafists allow that rabbis can change matters and produce somewhat superficial formulaic ways of justifying what they knew intuitively was the way things ought to go. Whether or not Tosafists were correct in portraying the Talmud's rationale for Moses is not the point. They opened a way of reasoning allowing for the understanding of emendation and the continued practice of it. And they argued that the sincere changes are indeed how God would ultimately want things.

What Moses did on one scale, rabbis can do on another. Hence, the Talmud in several places says that principles of partitions, and interruptions, and forbidden amounts were *halakhah moshe mi-sinai* and in another place it says they are Scriptural and still other places assume they are creations of the Rabbis.[25] The Talmud claims the biblical derivations are not valid but only suggestive. When the rabbis determine whatever they determine in their own terms, they produce somewhat superficial textual arguments, not an iron tight exegesis. Still, one can legitimately proclaim these matters are in the category of divinely ordained laws given to Moses. That freedom was divinely granted. The Talmudic rabbis can imitate the way Moses decided law, on his decision, using, in some unorthodox fashion, textual indicators as support. Now that these matters have been decided in such a way they are accepted by God and are quasi divine law to the point that if they are not observed, the divine law is breached. The implications for a theology of this type might help blur the line between what the Rabbis saw as historical notions of legal development and absolute religious dictates of divine law. In certain cases when the Rabbis declare matters to be a certain way, they now define the divine law for all time. And when they decide a text must be read a certain way, even if the text is altered in so doing (to reconcile the canonized Baraita or Mishnah with the authoritative teaching of certain rabbis) that text will always read that way, albeit only in the *halakhic* minds of decisors.

Hence what Rav Moshe did is not so surprising. The danger in allowing such moves is a very high price to pay to maintain the consistent integrity of the system as envisioned by a scholar immersed twenty-four hours a day, seven days a week, in Torah study. Rav Moshe knew what was at stake and was willing to take the risks. Rabbi Waldenberg was not. Once we enter the road of dismissing the recorded tradition we enter a territory of slippery slopes and have to desist. This brings us to conclude that where gross errors are evident in a text we need not hesitate to emend within the text itself. Where emendations are called for because of reasons of logical impossibilities in the flow of the text, they are warranted. They should be indicated as corrected readings but the text should not be altered. In these cases we can claim we are re-establishing the original text. Where emendations happen for legal reasons, we should not touch any text but rather note the text requires correction in such and such a way since the *halakha* is definitely at odds with the text. The text is not supreme, the *halakha* is. *Halakha* is a product of much more than textual reasoning.

In conclusion then we can distinguish between some types of proposed emendations in rabbinic circles for ideological reasons and emendations based on textual grounds, including the need for coherence. But this distinction blurs at the edges in some cases as we can debate how far to push the idea of coherence. That is not to deny that there is tremendous danger in the emendation of texts and we do not suggest that emendation is a solution to making texts fit our tastes. We should be careful in thinking that emendation is the last refuge of the rogue, although sometimes it might be.

Talmudists had two approaches to solving textual difficulties: *pilpul* (strained exegesis) and emendation. There were those who would develop a hermeneutic to push the sense of a text to reveal meanings that yield historical and philosophic truths. Then there were those who would play with the wording of the text until it clearly said what one expected it should say. Rabbi Meir was a scribe in Tannaitic (prior to 200 CE) times who was warned by his teachers to be very, very careful for he could destroy the whole world with a slight tick of the quill (Eruvin 13a). The types of errors envisaged by the commentators as they explain this passage in the Talmud show us their awareness of copyist errors that even the most scrupulous scribe might inadvertently introduce. In turn the universal awareness of copyist errors made it very easy to imagine that manuscripts could be easily corrected without recourse to other manuscripts of the same work. Once corruptions entered texts they took on a life of their own. Since copyists did make errors the temptation to emend readings was ever present and scholars could easily rationalize their clever emendations of texts to produce cogent readings. The responsibility of the Rabbi to preserve the sacred tradition acted as a brake to the run-away possibilities of such freedom. But in the end, the structure and weight of the entire tradition circumscribed the firm boundaries beyond which no new or even old idea could pass.[26]

ENDNOTES

[1] I want to thank Herb Basser for discussing with me his research on similar topics, including the text of a talk he presented at the SBL in Orlando in 1998. He told me his early publications on rabbinic hermeneutics resulted in misuse of the information by Hebrew Christians. He suggested I post the following warning taken from Mark Twain's well-known prologue: "Persons attempting to find a motive in this narrative will be prosecuted; persons attempting to find a moral in it will be banished; persons attempting to find a plot will be shot."
[2] *Tradition and the Biological Revolution: The Application of Jewish Law to the Critically Ill,* Edinburgh, Edinburgh University Press, 1989. See p. 94 sec (e) and p. 95 sec (f).
[3] *Im eyno inyan lazeh tenehu inyan lazeh.* See, for instance, Mekhilta Bo 18, Sifra Vayikra Nedava, *parashah* 12, Sifra Zav Perek 12, *perek* 13, Sifre Beha'alotecha, piska 20.
[4] *Peshita* appears 914 times. For cases solved by emendation see , for instance, Eruvin 41a and Baba Kamma 17b.
[5] *Bameh devarim amurim* appears 54 times in Mishnah itself. See, for example, Peah 7, Kilaim 2, Shvi'it 3 and 4, Trumot 3.
[6] *Hacha bemai askinan* appears 435 times. Unless otherwise noted all citations to Talmud are to the Babylonina Talmud. See, for example, Berackhot 20b, 26a, 27a, Shabbat 15b, 45b.
[7] *Eima* appears 219 times. See, for example, Berakhot 5b, 8a, Shabbat 7b, Pesahim 81a.
[8] *Hasorei mihasera vehakhi ketanei* appears 34 times. See, for instance, Berakhot 13b, Shabbat 62b, pesahim 10b.
[9] *Sami (dal).* See, for example, Shabbat 14a, Peahim 104a, Zevahim 56a.
[10] *Muhlaf/ ipuh* appears 82 times. See, for example, Berakhot 25b, 44a, Shabbat 59a, 66a.
[11] See E. S. Rosenthal, "Tradition and Innovation in the Halakha of the Sages," *Tarbiz* 63 (1994) 321-74 [Hebrew with English abstract, xix-xx].
[12] *M'an detani...la mishtabesh* appears 34 times, dealing with words which had letters which were pronounced similarly and the words (having diferent meanings were interchanged). See, for instance, Eruvin 61a, Sukka 50b, Beitza 35b, Avodah Zarah 2a.
[13] *Trei tannai aliba de...* See, for example, Berakhot 3a, 52a, Betzah 32a, Ta'anit 4b.
[14] *I itmar hakhi itmar* appears 37 times. See, for example, Shabbat 39b,41b, 44a, 44b *etc.*
[15] *Lav beferush itmar eleh mihkhlala...*appears 13 times. See, for example, Berakhot 9a, Shabbat 29a, 146b, Babba Metzia 101a.
[16] Philo (*Hypothetica 7:6*) also says such derivations are to be accorded the status of written Scripture.
[17] That was considered boorish behavior.
[18] See *Shulchan Aruch* and commentaries, *Yoreh Deah* 279:1.
[19] See his *Sinopsis la-Talmud ha-Yerushalmi.* Tubingen: J.C.B. Mohr (Paul Siebeck) 1991 and his *Sinopsis le-sifrut ha-hekhalot. Tubingen:* J.C.B. Mohr (P. Siebeck) 1981.
[20] R.N.A. Rabbinovicz, *Dikdukei Sofrim,* Jerusalem, 1959/60.
[21] See *Tanhuma Beshalakh* 15:16 for a list of places it is suggested that the *Men of the Great Assembly* altered the wording of the Tanak. See also M. Zipor, "Some notes on the origin of the tradition of the eighteen 'tiqqune soperim,'" *Vetus Testamentum* 44 (1994): 77-102.
[22] See Yerushalmi Ta'anit 4:2.
[23] See the *baraita* in Yevamot 62a.
[24] See Tosafot to Shabbat 87a.

[25] See discussions in the talmudic commentaries to Eruvin 4a and Sukka 5b.

[26] The Rabbis (*Sifre Shoftim piska* 45) envisioned the integrity of the tradition, including the names of who said what, to be unassailable. They interpreted the prohibition to move boundary markers of neighbors to refer to making wanton changes in the received tradition. See E.E. Urbach, *The S ages: their concepts and beliefs*, Jerusalem, 1975: 291ff.

6

CHRISTIANITY'S PROBLEM WITH HISTORY AND ITS LESSONS FOR JUDAIC STUDIES

Donald Harman Akenson

A lecture given at the Institute for Judaic Studies,
Congregation Shaar Hashomayim, Montreal
May 2001

(1)

I am grateful for the opportunity to speak with serious people: careful students of Torah who take religious scholarship seriously. This gives me the luxury of being able to take a good deal of shared knowledge for granted and therefore to compress into a short space some very complex matters and to do so with the confidence that you will fill in the missing steps yourself.

To be able to do this affords me great relief. In my world, the trivialization of religion is endemic and somewhat enraging. In the last few years I've spent a fair amount of time in New Zealand, and I bring you this report. The religion department of the Victoria University of Wellington, NZ, has recently changed two course titles to more adequately reflect their substance. Now (1) the former World Religions course is called "From Jerusalem to Mecca via Rome." And (2) the former History of Christianity course is now offered as "Jesus and the Movies." Think about that.

I did not come here today to bad-mouth my own tradition, Christianity. Nor would I ask you to respect me if I did. However, I do wish to deal with one of Christianity's great problems.

The problem is history. Or, if you prefer, historicity, meaning in this case, historical accuracy in the secular sense: of events and utterances that are verifiable at a fairly high level of probability. This should be of some interest to you as educated people – history is the common thread of much civilized discourse – and also because to *some* (but not the same) degree, Judaism is also interested in historicity.

That said, Christianity as a belief system has a vulnerability that it does not share with Judaism. The traditional standpoint of Christianity is that the faith is dependent not simply upon Torah as the Word of the Almighty as explicated by the Teachers of the Faithful. It is also dependent upon Torah as being embodied in the actions of one individual, Yeshua of Nazareth. No Yeshua, no Christianity. Now, it is possible to draw all sorts of exegetical and theological arabesques around the figure of Yeshua – which can run from interpreting him as the Gospels do as the son of God, to "liberal" efforts to interpret his words as those of a slightly weird prophet. But all these approaches require one thing: an operational belief that we can recover with some degree of historical accuracy a portfolio of things that Yeshua did and said.

That's Christianity's great problem, *for it conflates the message and the messenger.* The Christian version of Torah cannot exist without reference to the specific voice of Yeshua. When I discussed this with Peter Mason, the bishop of Ontario (who very decently still considers me to be a good Anglican), he said "In Christianity, the messenger *is* the message."

My heart sank. He probably is right but, as I will suggest in a moment, we know very little about the messenger. And certainly not enough to suggest that all Torah is embodied in his actions and sayings, whatever they may have been.

So, what I would like to do in our very brief time together is (1) suggest in a bit more detail the degree of Christianity's vulnerability; (2) indicate that there have been some very intelligent attempts to deal with tlhe apparent paucity of evidence concerning Yeshua of Nazareth – these among a lot of bogus, silly, and downright contemptible pseudo-scholarship; and (3) that the best work of Christian scholars on historical issues, although it well may not solve Christianity's problem with history, has some nifty inside-moves that could be adapted so as to enrich the study of Judaism.

Here let me point you to a great semi-silence in the massive literature that is called The Quest of the Historical Jesus (that's the title of an amazing 1906 book by Albert Schweitzer): that the most important event in the history of Judaism from the Babylonian exile onwards – the Destruction of the Second Temple – is mentioned only in passing and virtually never as the great causal lever that led to Christianity's changing from an off-brand of Pharisaism, one of the dozens of Judaisms of the pre-Destruction era, into a religion of its own.

The Destruction forced the Yeshua-followers to do for themselves what the Rabbis were engaged in at Yavneh and later Usha: preserving the religion of the Temple, after the Temple had been destroyed. To put it another way, they had to create an invisible temple to replace the physical one. The Yeshua-followers do this after 70CE by turning Yeshua of Nazareth into something that would have surprised him – into Jesus-the-Christ. He is made a deity, an incarnation of Torah, a Paschal lamb, a blood sacrifice. Emerging Christianity ties all this to an idea that is relatively new in Judaism (and probably a minority view before the Destruction) – namely, the resurrection of the dead and judgement of the individual soul. And the idea of Moshiah is highjacked and redefined. Simultaneously, the Tanakh is retro-read as a prolegomena to Jesus-the-Christ's ministry. Thus, the New Testament is written using almost entirely motifs from the Tanakh, artfully rearranged, with the addition of some Jewish material from the later era that is not found in the Tanakh itself, particularly apocalyptic thought way past that even of the Book of Daniel in its sanguinary details.

The New Testament is an artistic and semantic triumph, but historically it's a mess. Everything in it, save the letters of St. Paul, is written *after* the transformation of Yeshua of Nazareth that follows upon the Destruction. Hence, to put it bluntly, the Gospels are lousy history. They are anonymous documents (the names of the alleged authors are put on the spines in mid-second century), they are not written (in the form we have them) by anyone who knew Yeshua of Nazareth, and only a small number of events have third party verification.

Let's very swiftly review the evidentiary situation. Begin with FIRST PARTY EVIDENCE: that is, data provided by the historical individual himself. There is none whatsoever. Yeshua left no manuscripts, letters, inscriptions. We do not know from his own hand a single thing he did or a single word he said. Fine: that's the case with a lot of historical figures, but we will need something else, obviously.

Next: THIRD PARTY EVIDENCE. That is: independent attestation from a source that is neither closely associated with the individual in question, nor an implacable enemy. One discovers that (with the inclusion of the Apostle Paul, for whom there is first-person evidence), of the people we encounter in the Christian scriptures, only four players are confirmed. (That's in addition to various Roman and civic officials who are essentially rentable props in the Christian drama.) The four are (1) Yeshua, who is certainly not fictional; (2) John-the-Baptizer, whom Herod Antipas puts to death; (3) Yacov, brother of Yeshua, who gets on the wrong side of the Temple establishment in the early 60s and is killed. And add to this (4) Paul, from whom we have seven authentic first-person letters. Real people, good evidence.

The rest (again, save for Paul's letters) is SECOND PARTY EVIDENCE. That is: material provided by people who were emotionally or ideologically attached to the Yeshua movement. Of the Gospels ask: what is there in them that deals with the relationship of these central people? Let's make it really bare-bones and limit the query to Yeshua and John-the-Baptizer. I think we can legitimately meld the second- and the third-party evidence to give the following schematic of the basic social physics of the earliest Yeshua-faith:

1. John-the-Baptizer was a Jewish prophet of the late second Temple era who used ritual cleansing as the motif of his ministry.

2. Yeshua of Nazareth was possibly his kinsman.

3. In any case, Yeshua's own religious animation came when he was baptized by John.

4. After undergoing John's version of the ritual mikveh, Yeshua became John's disciple.

5. Later, Yeshua amicably moved away from the Baptizer and began his own movement.

6. As two of the multiple Judaisms that swirled around in late Second Temple times, both Yeshua's and John's movements developed as rivals, but it appears they were sympathetic ones.

That is as far as we can go, using the Gospels, if we treat them like any other historical source – which as an historian I must do. A few actions, and no words from Yeshua himself. Yet, Christians have always taken the Gospels as the most trustworthy source of information on their Messenger.

There are only two ways to deal with the Gospels. One is to take them on faith. This can be done at varying levels of affirmation, but once one puts extra-rational or non-rational credence in the Christian texts, one becomes, in some sense, a Christian. And that's not an exercise we are here engaged in.

So, the alternative is to approach the texts forensically. Now, there is a great deal of very bad history done on this issue, but there is one set of forensic efforts that is suggestive by analogy for improving our understanding of Jewish texts. This is an attempt – now several centuries in train – to develop a STRATIGRAPHY of the documents on Yeshua. If it were possible to find within the Gospels elements that were pre-Destruction – that is, elements that were not affected by the radical change in world conditions, and thus in world view, that resulted in the Yeshua-faith moving outside of Judaism – then we could possibly gain some knowledge of what Yeshua thought of himself and how he defined Torah.

The most useful of these forensic efforts focuses on what is called "The Synoptic Puzzle." I wish we had several hours to look at this because if you like elegant reasoning this is a great puzzle to play with. (It's covered in detail schematically in my *Saint Saul. A Skeleton Key to the Historical Jesus.*) The puzzle is this. The three synoptic gospels – Matthew, Mark and Luke, called "synoptic," meaning having similar optics – have a great deal of overlap. And at times, two agree with each other against the third, but not in an obvious pattern. So, somebody copied somebody else.

To grossly simplify, what usually comes out of the scholarly mill is this:

– Matthew and Luke
\ /
copied a lot of
\ /
Mark

– But Matthew and Luke have a lot in common
\ /
that comes from an unknown source called
\ /
Q

So it is conceivable that some of the material about Yeshua found in Q is pre-Destruction. The real Jesus, maybe.

(2)

You might think that at this point I'm going to tell you the Big Truth. No: at this point in our discussion I am going to change direction abruptly. Let's forget Christianity for a few minutes except to suggest that if one adapted some of the attitudes and techniques of the best scholars of early Christianity (incidentally, increasingly these are Jewish scholars) to the study of the texts that start to be formed in the same era as the Gospels (the immediate post-Destruction era), then one might enrich one's understanding of early Rabbinic thought and history. The key here is that this can be done without the risk to Judaism that the parallel effort exposes Christianity to. Specifically, Torah in the Rabbinic texts does not depend on any single voice. Nor is the truth of Torah dependent upon its being carried by any given messenger. So, it's a low risk enterprise – and anything that deepens our understanding of the Faith is high reward. Low risk, high reward.

(The one exception to this low-risk, high-reward situation is if you happen to believe that all Rabbinic thought and all study of Torah is invalid if one does not believe that the Pentateuch came directly and inviolably from the hand of Moses and that all fundamental Oral Torah was uttered directly by Moses and transmitted inerrantly down the generations. That makes the message of Torah dependent upon its being touched by a specific messenger. Obviously, such a belief is similar to the Christian conflation of message and messenger and would lead Rabbinic Judaism to have essentially the same problems with historicity that Christianity does. Few of you, I suspect, are Biblical or Auricular Fundamentalists.)

Would it not be rewarding to have a stratigraphy of Rabbinic thought? Rewarding because it would give us greater historical understanding; rewarding because we would read the Rabbis better if we knew what they had read (or heard) before they made their own arguments; and rewarding in a cosmic sense (if I may presume) in that the basic doctrine underlying Judaism is that the Almighty unrolls His work and will in human time. If we see how the Faith has developed over time, it is like watching a drawing being made by a pen whose tip is visible, but nothing else. Yet, as the drawing emerges, we learn a great deal about the Unseen Hand.

Ideally this stratigraphy of Rabbinic thought would have two aspects. The first and easiest is cross-textual: which items came first, second, etc. and which ones were used by the author-editors of later texts and in what way. To me one of the most curious things about Judaic studies is that when I set out to read the Rabbinic corpus, I could find no single discussion of this matter. Yet this seems to me to be the most basic issue, something one would teach students before sending them into the documents themselves. The chart that I gave you last time that I visited with you is my own view of the matter. It's not highly controversial, just basic. (It is based mostly on the brilliant pioneering work of Professor Jacob Neusner.)

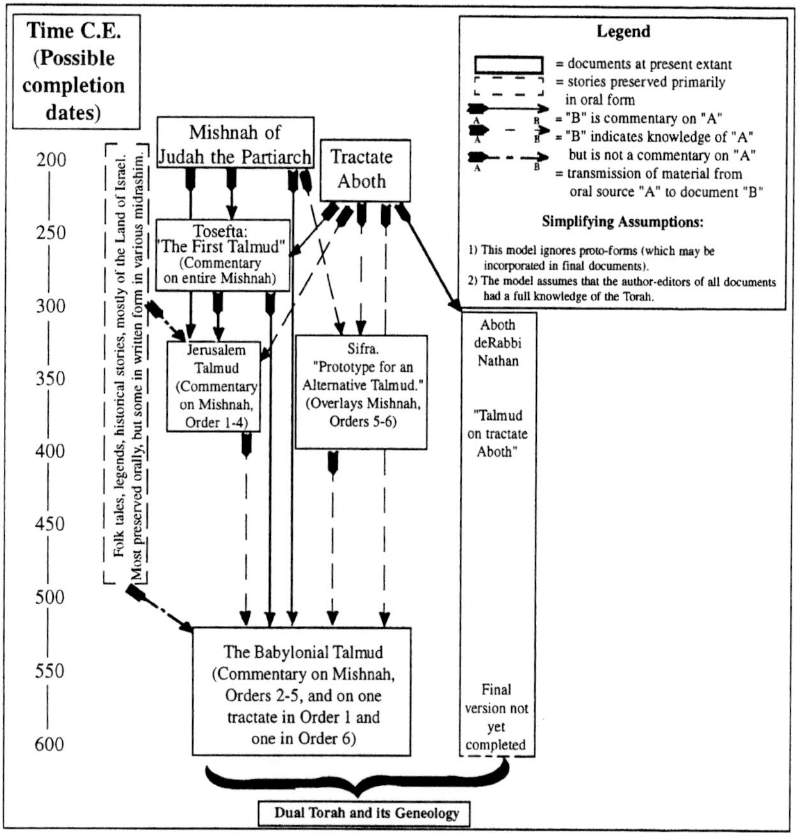

Much more difficult is to determine the stratigraphy *within* any given Rabbinic document. Each of these documents developed over 100 years, minimum, and several of them took hundreds of years. So there obviously was an evolutionary process in each one. Some ideas came before others; some ideas are reactions to earlier ones. The actual task will take great technical virtuosity, but the questions that must be assayed are very simple. In my view they are:

(1) What is the character of the manuscript base that underlies each document? Mishnah, Tosefta, Sifra, Yerushalmi, Bavli? This is not an impious question. One does truth no service by simply declaring our present transcriptions to be accurate. The Almighty, in His wisdom, allows even the whole earth to wobble a little bit. It is a little unnerving to realize that there is not anything approaching a critical edition for any of the core texts. That is: an edition which presents all the variant manuscript and printed readings and adjudges as between them and explains why.

(2) Does each document testify to anything but the views of the final editor or editors? That is the single biggest question. If the answer is no, then no stratigraphy within any document is possible. Now, we can break that big query down into smaller ones.

(3) So our third question is: do the texts report literally and accurately everything everybody said? If yes, then, all we would have to do is arrange the various arguments in sequential order. The difficulty here is that the variant manuscript traditions testify to some imperfections; and, in any case, the way the texts sound is a real problem. Each of the major items is in one voice. The voices of the living Rabbis have been flattened out, placed in a single register.

(4) Therefore, a more productive query is: do the texts quote *anyone* accurately? Do they represent anyone *ipsissima verba*?

(5) If we assume for the sake of argument that at least some of the sayings attributed to the Sages of Blessed Memory are verbally accurate, then how does one separate the verbally accurate reports from those that are not? Thus far no scholar has developed a reliable filter, but that does not say it is impossible, just very difficult.

(6) Are the *stam* – the anonymous sayings not ascribed to any specific Sage found in several texts – the interpolations of the final editor (and thus the top layer) or do they represent the earliest material, items so old that it has been forgotten who said them?

(7) Are we better off to adopt the strategy of suggesting that, although we cannot decipher at present which quotations are dead-accurate, we can take them as being a good indication of the particular Sage's views in a general way. This is a huge matter of dispute for historians of Rabbinic thought and I can only warn you that traditional Orthodox thought (which accepts the reliability of attributions as a matter of faith) runs into *un*traditional Orthodox and every other kind of thought on this. This is not an issue easily settled.

(8) Might we be farther along if we forgot attributions altogether and looked at idea-units on their own? There may be a stratigraphy, an evolution of thought, that is apparent once one erases the names attached to the idea-traits. And since most forms of Judaism do not confuse the messenger with the message, we could see evolution of Torah clearly.

Now, why am I pushing so hard on this? For all the reasons I mentioned earlier and for one other: in chronicling the development of Rabbinic Judaism we have the same intellectual problem that we have with chronicling early Christianity. Namely: all the Rabbinic texts in the form that we at present have them were produced after that forever mind-bending moment, the Destruction. If we want to understand Jewish origins, then it would be of immense value to find within the texts (especially within the Mishnah) the pre-Destruction Pharisaic beliefs that evolved into Rabbinic Judaism. It may be time for someone to re-do the present *meisterwerk* on the topic, Jacob Neusner's *The Rabbinic Traditions about the Pharisees Before 70* (1971). That is a monumental work and the rewards of revisiting it would be great.

(3)

You probably know that ever since Archbishop Cranmer read Aristotle, every talk or sermon given by a Protestant has been divided into three parts.

First, I suggested Christianity's historical problem and some ways scholars have tried to deal with it; secondly, the usefulness of learning a few technical tricks to employ in chronicling an evolutionary trajectory for earliest Rabbinic Judaism; now, thirdly, I wish to bring us back to Christianity's problem.

It is time to eschew what Norman Davies refers to as "the false philosophy of opposites" in the exploration of the complexities of Christian and Jewish histories. Specifically, I think the most fruitful (relatively) untapped source for the history of pre-Destruction and early post-Destruction Judaism is the so-called New Testament. If read critically. And, horrors, the most revealing of all about Judaism is the one writer most despised by most Jews: Saul of Tarsus who emerges as Saint Paul in Christian tradition.

Before you pelt me, let me telegraph the primary inference for Christian readers that comes out of my book *Saint Saul*. This is that the "New Testament" contains very little about the teaching or life of Yeshua of Nazareth that a secular historian would say has a probability of being accurate. Just as in the billions of planets in the universe there is a strong probability of intelligent life somewhere in the universe other than on earth, so in the Christian scriptures some of the acts and sayings attributed to Yeshua are apt to be accurate. Yet, just as our chances of detecting intelligent life on other planets are virtually (but not quite) zero, so our chances of determining the authentic sayings and actions of Yeshua are extremely low.

The paradox here is that the so-called New Testament turns out to yield more useful material on Jewish history in the late pre-Destruction period than it does on early Christian history.

Sometime read Saint Paul's seven authentic letters (1 Thessalonians, 1 and 2 Corinthians, Philippians, Philemon, Galatians, Romans). Try to prescind what you know you will hate about them. Instead accept what Rabbi Samuel Sandmel said, that Paul is the only diaspora-Pharisee we know. In fact, he and Philo of Alexandria (the first Jewish theologian according to some) are the only two Jews of the late Second Temple era who have given us their theological opinions in their own words and their own hand. One excludes Josephus, who is no theologian. And Philo, also a diaspora-Jew, is a semi-Platonic philosopher who is brilliant, but a long way from the Rabbis. Paul is closer.

Because of our limited time, I will suggest only one thing you might watch. It is Paul's use of language. It can be Billingsgate, when he is vexed, especially when disciplining local churches that are going off the rails, but when he is on, when he is dictating arguments that are like the sermons he preached in synagogues all over Asia Minor, then he is sublime. As pieces of rhetorical art, look at the letter to the Romans and at the 13th chapter of First Corinthians. They are artistic masterpieces.

Then compare them *stylistically* to the argument on any topic in the Mishnah. The Rabbis come out sounding very intelligent, but abrupt, inelegant, disputatious, contradictive of each other, and often they are intellectually victorious without being at all convincing: because for an argument to be convincing it not only has to be intellectually powerful, it has to be seductive, it has to make the listener want to embrace it.

Was Paul smarter than the Rabbis? Heavens no! I doubt if he would have had a seat farther forward at Yavneh than the back row. But he shows us a probable characteristic of the early Rabbis that the Mishnah and Talmuds necessarily elide. This is that the Rabbis were not merely brilliant slicers of Halakah, but when met with face to face – when they gave uninterrupted lectures or meditations – they were men of immense subtlety, of admirable ability in the use of metaphor and of captivating figures of speech. They could be so convincing that we would embrace their ideals and wrap our entire life in them.

We are not aware of these abilities, I think, because of the way their ideas were preserved over long periods of time: in memory. This meant that Rabbinic thought had to be reduced to mnemonic units that are telegraphic in quality. What was necessarily lost was the evidence of rhetorical skills that were as strong and subtle as those anywhere in the world of Greek and Roman rhetoric. It was this rhetorical skill among the proto-Rabbis and Rabbis that made possible what Louis Feldman has delineated as a great missionary movement among the non-Jews in the first two or three centuries of the Common Era. Paul confirms that skill.

Let us, in the spirit of generous experimentation, give Paul the last word:

> *Though I speak with the tongues of men and of angels, and have not love, I am become as sounding brass, or a tinkling cymbal.*
>
> *And though I have the gift of prophecy, and understand all mysteries, and all knowledge; and though I have all faith, so that I could remove mountains, and have not love, I am nothing.*
>
> *And though I bestow all my goods to feed the poor, and though I give my body to be burned, and have not love, it profiteth me nothing.*
>
> *Love suffereth long, and is kind; love envieth not; love vaunteth not itself, is not puffed up;*
>
> *Doth not behave itself unseemly, seeketh not her own, is not easily provoked, thinketh no evil;*
>
> *Rejoiceth not in iniquity, but rejoiceth in the truth;*
>
> *Beareth all things, believeth all things, hopeth all things, endureth all things.*
>
> *Love never faileth: but whether there be prophecies, they shall fail; whether there be tongues, they shall cease; whether there be knowledge, it shall vanish away.*
>
> *For now we know in part, and we prophesy in part.*
>
> *But when that which is perfect is come, then that which is in part shall be done away.*
>
> *When I was a child, I spake as a child, I understood as a child, I thought as a child: but when I became a man, I put away childish things.*
>
> *For now we see through a glass, darkly; but then face to face: now I know in part; but then shall I know even as also I am known.*
>
> *And now abideth faith, hope, love, these three; but the greatest of these is love.*

That, in timbre, meter, subtlety, and force is an authentic Jewish voice. But that's only my opinion.

7

What, Exactly, Is Israel's Gentile Problem? Rabbinic Perspectives on Galatians 2

JACOB NEUSNER

All Judaisms have to define the "Israel" of which they speak — that is, that social entity of which Scripture speaks and which is embodied in that very Judaism's social order — and, in consequence, each Judaism has also to propose a final solution to the gentile problem.[1] It has, in other words, to explain to itself who gentiles are and why they matter. And that explanation will embody the deepest systemic concerns, the generative commitment, of that Judaism. For in the account of who we are and who they are the system identifies what counts. Not only so, but when we wish to compare one Judaism with another, we may take as our arena for comparison and contrast the doctrines of Israel and the gentile set forth by each, for these will attest to the character of the whole of the respective Judaisms.

A certain logic will guide thought on the matter. If the system focuses upon issues of sanctification, as is the case at Qumran and for the Pharisees represented by the Gospels and most of the Rabbinic traditions pertinent to the period before 70, then gentiles will represent the ultimate embodiment of uncleanness, the opposite of the holy. If the system focuses upon issues of salvation, as in the case of Paul's system and that of the sages of the Rabbinic documents seen whole, then gentiles will come to be classified as the un-saved, Israel, those en route to salvation. And, it will follow, a Judaic system that concerns itself with sanctification will identify the final solution of the gentile problem as a matter of exclusion, especially from meals, where issues of sanctification come to realization. A Judaic system of salvation will dismiss as inconsequential the matter of eating

[1] Lecture at the Bard College Institute of Advanced Theology conference on James and Peter and Paul, held in Boston, Mass., Nov. 20, 1999, in conjunction with the national meetings of the Society of Biblical Literature and the American Academy of Religion.

with gentiles. That is gentiles bear consequences of another kind altogether; they stand for different things; they form a counterpart and opposite of Israel on different grounds altogether.

I

The initial Christian systems within the Israelite framework — systems that appeal to the Scriptures of ancient Israel and that deem the social category, "Israel" of the ancient Scriptures to be realized in the community of Christ formed in the here and now — follow suit.[2] They realize the same dichotomy and replicate the same consequences. The one system defines the gentile problem in terms of uncleanness because at stake is Israel's sanctification, the other, in terms of sin and atonement, because the issue is salvation. This we see in the framing of the gentile problem by the principals, James and Paul. When, in his letter to the Galatians, Paul reviews the three positions on eating with gentiles — James's, Peter's, and his own — I shall show, Paul frames Israel's gentile problem in a manner quite coherent with the Rabbinic sages' later definition of the same matter. What renders the gentiles an issue defines what is at stake in the larger systemic formations adumbrated in Paul's account of matters: gentiles matter at meals, gentiles matter at the end of days — with strikingly different consequences in the here and now.

James stresses that Israelites are not to eat with gentiles, and we do not assume too much if we explain his position by appeal to purity-laws. Gentiles are cultically unclean, on a continuum with corpses, and anyone who wishes to eat his ordinary meals in a manner befitting the kingdom of priests and the holy people will not sit at table with them. Peter's position is ambiguous. It is Paul's formulation of the matter that entirely shifts the ground of argument, away from purity altogether and toward the matter of salvation, so in a famous passage:

> We...know that a man is not justified by works of the law but through faith in Jesus Christ, even we have believed in Christ Jesus in order to be justified by faith in Christ and not by works of the law, because by works of the law shall no one be justified.
>
> Galatians 2:15-16

Now if we ask what keeping cultic cleanness has to do with salvation ("being reckoned righteous"), the answer is, nothing. The two Christian systems scarcely intersect; each works out the dialectics of its own logic: the oppositions of Israel and gentiles on its own grounds. If uncleanness counts, then the gentiles form an ontological, not an eschatological category, having to do with sanctification in the here and now. Paul's gentile problem has to do with salvation, whether for Israel or for gentiles, because Paul's system is a salvific system, and not because it is an alternative, within the same category-formation, to James's (or Peter's, whatever

---

[2] The present formulation accommodates Catholic Christianity and eliminates the Gnostic.

that can have been). In Galatians we have no argument between persons who share the same premises and differ as to detail — that is to say, a true argument. We witness, rather, a collision of closed systems, the one unable to comprehend the category-formations that define, for the other, the selection and interpretation of the facts to begin with.

Then in shifting the focus from relationships to gentiles to salvation, Paul has simply re-categorized the matter of keeping cultic cleanness. Relationships to gentiles no longer define the focus of discourse, as James and Peter maintain, because in the most material terms possible, eating with them bears no consequence. What counts is salvation, and in that framework, gentiles and Israelites share a common past and a common future. To state matters more simply, there is no reading Galatians 2 outside of the framework of Romans 9-11, where Paul presents a final solution to the gentile problem in his definition of Israel: "not all who are descended from Israel belong to Israel, and not all are children of Abraham because they are his descendants. It is not the children of the flesh who are the children of God, but the children of the promise are reckoned as descendants" (Romans 9:6-8, among many passages).

II

For the theological system that animates the Rabbinic writings of antiquity, Mishnah, Tosefta, Yerushalmi, Bavli, and Midrash-compilations, in response to the Written Torah, Israel stands for those who will stand in judgment and enter eternal life, and gentiles stand for those who will not. The systemic logic concerns itself with the salvation of Israel in the end of days through the sanctification of Israel in the here and now. When the Mishnah states, "All Israel has a portion of the world to come" (with some minor exceptions), it invites a transposition of predicate and subject: "those who have a portion in the world to come" are encompassed within Israel. They are those who acknowledge one God, who is made manifest in the Torah. Paul and the Rabbinic sages concur that birth within Israel, not only coming under the wings of God's presence and accepting God's dominion in the Torah, counts too, Paul's formulation in Romans exploring the logical requirements of the problem he has taken for himself. But if those who have a portion in the world to come are Israel, then who and what are gentiles? For the sages, the gentiles are those who have rejected the Torah. And that matters because it is through the Torah that God has made possible the regeneration of Adam. The Torah addresses the flaw in Adam that Eden revealed and announces the remedy: "The All-Merciful desires the heart."

III

Let me then state the Rabbinic doctrine of the gentiles. My exposition will leave no doubt of the systemic congruity of Paul's and the sages' definition of the category-formation, Israel/gentiles. For both systems, to be a gentile is to be a sinner, in the model of Adam and Eve, and to require a medium of regeneration from the human condition of rebellion against God. Paul in so many words refers to himself and Peter in the language: "We ourselves who are Jews by birth and not gentile sinners." Where Paul and sages part company it is whether or not the Torah serves as the medium of regeneration, which is to say, attaining that condition that will mark the person as "reckoned righteous." Sages will not use the language of justification, but their entire system is aimed at the transformation of humanity into Israel: those who know God and obey him. That is what embodies God's grace: the revelation of the Torah to Israel.

The Rabbinic doctrine of God defines Gentiles as idolaters, and Israelites worship the one, true God, who has made himself known in the Torah. What makes Israel Israel is the Torah. In the Oral Torah, that is the difference — the only consequential distinction — between Israel and the gentiles. Still, there is that and one other, Israel stands for life, the gentiles for death. That is because Israel will stand in judgment — the Rabbinic counterpart to the language of justification — and the gentiles will not. Before proceeding, let us consider a clear statement of why idolatry defines the boundary between Israel and everybody else. The reason is that idolatry — rebellious arrogance against God — encompasses the entire Torah. The religious duty to avoid idolatry is primary; if one violates the religious duties, he breaks the yoke of commandments, and if he violates that single religious duty, he violates the entire Torah. Violating the prohibition against idolatry is equivalent to transgressing all Ten Commandments:

SIFRÉ TO NUMBERS CXI:I.1FF.

1. A. "But if you err and do not observe [all these commandments which the Lord has spoken to Moses" (Num. 15:22-26):
2. A. "But if you err and do not observe:"
   B. *Scripture speaks of idolatry.*

Now we test the proposition, as sages commonly do, by proposing other readings of the evidence that is adduced besides the one offered as normative. Here is a sequence of options:

C. You maintain that Scripture speaks of idolatry. But perhaps Scripture refers to any of the religious duties that are listed in the Torah?

D. Scripture states, "...then if it was done unwittingly without the knowledge of the congregation." Scripture thereby has singled out a particular religious duty unto itself, and what might that be? It is the prohibition against idolatry.

E. You maintain that Scripture speaks of idolatry. But perhaps Scripture refers to any of the religious duties that are listed in the Torah?

F. Scripture states, "But if you err and do not observe," indicating that all of the religious duties come together to give testimony concerning a single religious duty.

G. Just as if someone violates all of the religious duties, he thereby breaks off the yoke [of the commandments] and wipes out the mark of the covenant and so treats the Torah impudently, so if one violates a single religious duty, he thereby breaks off the yoke [of the commandments] and wipes out the mark of the covenant and so treats the Torah impudently.

H. And what might that single religious duty be? It is idolatry, for it is said [in that regard], "...to violate his covenant" (Deut. 17:2). [Thus the covenant refers in particular to the rule against idolatry, which then stands for the whole.]

I. "Covenant" moreover refers only to the Torah, as it is said, "These are the words of the covenant" (Deut. 28:69).

The systematic proof having been completed, we now pursue a different path to the same goal:

J. [Providing a different proof for the same proposition as D-I], Rabbi says, "Here the word 'all' is used, and elsewhere the word 'all' is used. Just as in the word 'all' used elsewhere Scripture refers to idolatry, so in the word 'all' used here Scripture refers to idolatry."

Now we show that idolatry requires the denial of the Ten Commandments:

3. A. "...which the Lord has spoken to Moses:"

B. How do you know that whoever confesses to belief in idolatry denies the Ten Commandments?

C. Scripture says, "...which the Lord has spoken to Moses," and elsewhere, "And God spoke all these words, saying" (Ex. 20:1). "God spoke one word..." (Ps. 62:12). "Are not my words like fire, says the Lord" (Jer. 23:29). So too in respect to that concerning which Moses was commanded Scripture says, "...all that the Lord God commanded through the hand of Moses."

D. How do we know that that same rule applies also to all matters concerning which the prophets were commanded?

E. Scripture says, "...from the day that the Lord gave commandment [and onward throughout your generations]."
F. And how do we know that that is the case also concerning the commandments entrusted to the patriarchs?
G. Scripture says, "...and onward throughout your generations."
H. And whence did the Holy One, blessed be he, begin to entrust commandments to the patriarchs?
I. As it is said, "And the Lord God commanded Adam" (Gen. 2:16).
J. Scripture thereby indicates that whoever confesses to belief in idolatry denies the Ten Commandments and rejects all of the commandments entrusted to Moses, the prophets, and the patriarchs.
K. And whoever denies idolatry confesses to belief in the entirety of the Torah.

Violating the religious duties in general means breaking the yoke of the commandments, but there is one that carries in its wake the violation of the entire Torah or all Ten Commandments. Idolatry is that one. And that is what defines gentiles, that is, the whole of humanity that does not know God.

To state matters in more general terms: in the theology of the Rabbinic sages, the category, the gentiles or the nations, without elaborate differentiation, encompasses all who are not-Israelites, that is, who do not belong to Israel and therefore do not know and serve God. That category takes on meaning only as complement and opposite to its generative counterpart, having no standing — self-defining characteristics — on its own. That is, since Israel encompasses the sector of humanity that knows and serves God by reason of God's self-manifestation in the Torah, the gentiles are comprised by everybody else: those placed by their own intention and active decision beyond the limits of God's revelation. Guided by the Torah Israel worships God, without its illumination gentiles worship idols. At the outset, therefore, the main point registers: by "gentiles" sages understand, God's enemies, and by "Israel" sages understand, those who know God as God has made himself known, which is, through the Torah. In no way do we deal with secular categories, but with theological ones.

The gentiles hate Israel and therefore hate God. What accounts for the logic that links the one to the other? The answer to that question fully spells out the doctrine of the gentiles that the Oral Torah constructs, and everything else is commentary. What defines the gentiles — the lack of the Torah — explains also why their very character requires them to hate Israel, the people of the Torah. The gentiles' hatred of Israel came about because of the revelation of the Torah at Sinai:

Bavli tractate Shabbat 9:3-4 I.45-6/89a

A. Said one of the rabbis to R. Kahana, "Have you heard the meaning of the words 'Mount Sinai'?"
B. He said to him, "The mountain on which miracles [nissim] were done for Israel."
C. "But then the name should be, Mount Nisai."
D. "Rather, the mountain on which a good omen was done for Israel."
E. "But then the name should be, Mount Sinai."
F. He said to him, "So why don't you hang out at the household of R. Pappa and R. Huna b. R. Joshua, for they're the ones who really look into lore."
G. For both of them say, "What is the meaning of the name, Mount Sinai? It is the mountain from which hatred [sinah] descended for the gentiles."

The key to the entire system — the Torah — opens the lock at hand. Israel accepts the Torah, gentiles reject it, and everything follows from that single fact. Israel knows God, gentiles deny him, and relations between the two sectors of humanity are determined by that fact.

Who, speaking categorically not historically, indeed are these "non-Israelites," called gentiles ("the nations," "the peoples," and the like)? The answer is dictated by the form of the question: who exactly is a "non-Israelite"? Then the answer concerning the signified is always relative to its signifier, Israel? Within humanity-other-than-Israel, differentiation articulates itself along gross, political lines, always in relationship to Israel. If humanity is differentiated politically, then, it is a differentiation imposed by what has happened between a differentiated portion of humanity and Israel. It is, then, that segment of humanity that under given circumstances has interacted with Israel: [1] Israel arising at the end and climax of the class of world empires, Babylonia, Media, Greece, Rome; or [2] Israel against Egypt; or [3] Israel against Canaan. That is the point at which Babylonia, Media, Greece, Rome, Egypt, or Canaan take a place in the narrative, become actors for the moment, but never givens, never enduring native categories. Then, when politics does not impose its structure of power-relationships, then humanity is divided between Israel and everyone else.

Gentile-idolaters and Israelite worshippers of the one and only God part company at death. Israelites die and rise from the grave, gentiles die and remain there. The roads intersect at the grave, each component of humanity taking its own path beyond. Israelites — meaning, those possessed of right conviction — will rise from the grave, stand in judgment (along with some gentiles, as we shall see in a moment), but then enter upon eternal life, to which no one else will enjoy access.

So, in substance, humanity viewed whole is divided between those who get a share in the world to come — Israel — and who will stand when subject to divine judgment and those who will not. These are extreme propositions. How do sages say what I impute to them, which is, to be Israel is to live forever, and to be gentile is to die once and for all time, so that, at the end of days God will save Israel and destroy idolatry? Here is one such formulation:

Bavli tractate Abodah Zarah 1:1 I:7-8, 10/4a

I.7 A. R. Hinena bar Pappa contrasted verses of Scripture: "It is written, 'As to the almighty, we do not find him exercising plenteous power' (Job 37:23), but by contrast, 'Great is our Lord and of abundant power' (Ps. 147:5), and further, 'Your right hand, Lord, is glorious in power' (Ex. 15:6).

B. "But there is no contradiction between the first and second and third statements, for the former speaks of the time of judgment [when justice is tempered with mercy, so God does not do what he could] and the latter two statements refer to a time of war [of God against his enemies]."

I.8 A. R. Hama bar Hanina contrasted verses of Scripture: "It is written, 'Fury is not in me' (Is. 27:4) but also 'The Lord revenges and is furious' (Nah. 1:2).

B. "But there is no contradiction between the first and second statements, for the former speaks of Israel, the latter of the gentiles."

C. R. Hinena bar Pappa said, "'Fury is not in me' (Is. 27:4), for I have already taken an oath: 'would that I had not so vowed, then as the briars and thorns in flame would I with one step burn it altogether.'"

I.10 A. That is in line with what Raba said, "What is the meaning of the verse, 'Howbeit he will not stretch out a hand for a ruinous heap though they cry in his destruction' (Job 30:24)?

B. "Said the Holy One, blessed be He, to Israel, 'When I judge Israel, I shall not judge them as I do the gentiles, for it is written, "I will overturn, overturn, overturn it" (Ezek. 21:32), rather, I shall exact punishment from them as a hen pecks.'

C. "Another matter: 'Even if the Israelites do not carry out a religious duty before me more than a hen pecking at a rubbish heap, I shall join together [all the little pecks] into a great sum: "although they pick little they are saved" (Job 30:24).

So I cannot over-stress the given on which all else is built: to be a gentile is to practice idolatry and to die, and to be Israel is to serve the one true God and to rise from the grave. That principle governs throughout. Everything else flows from it, and, in due course we shall see, upon that basis the present condition of the world is shown to cohere with the principle of the moral order of justice that prevails.

How does this conviction, already adumbrated in my definition of Israel play itself out? That the world to come opens before Israel is explicit, as in the opening statement of the Mishnah-treatise on the subject, Mishnah-tractate Sanhedrin 11:1A: "All Israelites have a share in the world to come, as it is said, 'Your people also shall be all righteous, they shall inherit the land forever; the branch of my planting, the work of my hands, that I may be glorified' (Is. 60:21).". But in that very context we recall, not even all Israel enters in. The ones who do not find definition in the logic of the Rabbinic sages viewed whole: those who deny the normative principles of the faith — that the Torah comes from Heaven, that the teaching of the resurrection of the dead derives from the Torah — lose out, for by their own word they do not know God, so, while remaining Israel, join the gentiles before the very gate of the world to come. So too the principle of measure for measure furthermore applies: those who deny resurrection as a principle of the Torah — the sole source of truth so far as sages are concerned — also do not get it.

This brings us from the principles to the details of sages' theology of the gentiles. What specifically do we know in the Torah about the gentiles? First, all those prior to Noah simply are wiped out, do not get a share in the world to come, and do not stand in Judgment. As to those after the flood, while they have no share in the world to come, they will stand in judgment. Justified, they still do not enter the world to come:

Mishnah-tractate Sanhedrin 11:3A-CC

A. The generation of the flood has no share in the world to come,
B. and they shall not stand in the judgment,
C. since it is written, "My spirit shall not judge with man forever" (Gen. 6:3)
D. neither judgment nor spirit.

Once the generation of the flood enters, it draws in its wake the generation of the dispersion and the men of Sodom:

E. The generation of the dispersion has no share in the world to come,
F. since it is said, "So the Lord scattered them abroad from there upon the face of the whole earth" (Gen. 11:8).

G. "So the Lord scattered them abroad" — in this world,
H. "and the Lord scattered them from there" — in the world to come.
I. The men of Sodom have no portion in the world to come,
J. since it is said, "Now the men of Sodom were wicked and sinners against the Lord exceedingly" (Gen. 13:13)
K. "Wicked" — in this world,
L. "And sinners" — in the world to come.
M. But they will stand in judgment.
N. R. Nehemiah says, "Both these and those will not stand in judgment,
O. "for it is said, 'Therefore the wicked shall not stand in judgment [108A], nor sinners in the congregation of the righteous' (Ps. 1:5)
P. 'Therefore the wicked shall not stand in judgment' — this refers to the generation of the flood.
Q. 'Nor sinners in the congregation of the righteous' — this refers to the men of Sodom."
R. They said to him, "They will not stand in the congregation of the righteous, but they will stand in the congregation of the sinners."

Now we shift to Israelite sinners, three classes of persons, with the same result: here too, some stand in judgment but will not enter the world to come. The spies who rejected the Land, the generation of the golden calf, condemned to die in the wilderness, and the party of Korah define the Israelites who lose out. They are those who rejected the restoration to the Land do not reenter the land at the restoration that commences with resurrection, those who opted for an idol instead of God, and those who rejected the Torah of Moses. So these classes of Israelites match the gentiles, for they deny the three principal components of salvation and redemption: restoration, service of one God, and acceptance of the authority of the Torah of Sinai; we note that some opinion differs, but the anonymous opinion represents the consensus of sages, as always:

S. The spies have no portion in the world to come,
T. as it is said, "Even those men who brought up an evil report of the land died by the plague before the Lord" (Num. 14:37)
U. "Died" — in this world.
V. "By the plague" — in the world to come.
W. "The generation of the wilderness has no portion in the world to come and will not stand in judgment,

X. "for it is written, 'In this wilderness they shall be consumed and there they shall die' (Num. 14:35), "The words of R. Aqiba.

Y. R. Eliezer says, "Concerning them it says, 'Gather my saints together to me, those that have made a covenant with me by sacrifice' (Ps. 50:5)."

Z. "The party of Korah is not destined to rise up,

AA. "for it is written, 'And the earth closed upon them' — in this world.

BB. "'And they perished from among the assembly' — in the world to come," the words of R. Aqiba.

CC. And R. Eliezer says, "Concerning them it says, 'The Lord kills and resurrects, brings down to Sheol and brings up again' (1 Sam. 2:6)."

The Mishnah then takes up special cases of particular classes of gentiles singled out by Scripture.

What about gentiles in general? All depends upon their own actions. Since the point of differentiation is idolatry as against worship of the one God, gentiles may enter into the category of Israel, which is to say, they recognize the one God and come to serve him. That means, whether now or later, some, perhaps many, gentiles will enter Israel, being defined as other Israelites are defined: those who worship the one and only God. The gentiles include many righteous persons. But by the end of days these God will bring to Israel:

Yerushalmi Berakhot 2:8 I:2:

A. When R. Hiyya bar Adda, the nephew of Bar Qappara, died Resh Laqish accepted [condolences] on his account because he [Resh Laqish] had been his teacher. We may say that [this action is justified because] a person's student is as beloved to him as his son.

B. And he [Resh Laqish] expounded concerning him [Hiyya] this verse: "My beloved has gone down to his garden, to the bed of spices, to pasture his flock in the gardens, and to gather lilies" [Song 6:2]. It is not necessary [for the verse to mention, 'To the bed of spices']. [It is redundant if you interpret the verse literally, for most gardens have spice beds.]

C. Rather [interpret the verse as follows:] My beloved — this is God; has gone down to his garden — this is the world; to the beds of spices — this is Israel; to pasture his flock in the gardens — these are the nations of the world; and to gather lilies — these are the righteous whom he takes from their midst.

Now a parable restates the proposition in narrative terms; having chosen a different mode of discourse from the narrative one that dominates in the Authorized History, Genesis through Kings, sages reintroduce narrative for an other-than-historical purpose, as here:

D. They offer a parable [relevant to this subject]. To what may we compare this matter [of the tragic death of his student]? A king had a son who was very beloved to him. What did the king do? He planted an orchard for him.

E. As long as the son acted according to his father's will, he would search throughout the world to seek the beautiful saplings of the world, and to plant them in his orchard. And when his son angered him he went and cut down all his saplings.

F. Accordingly, so long as Israel acts according to God's will he searches throughout the world to seek the righteous persons of the nations of the world and bring them and join them to Israel, as he did with Jethro and Rahab. And when they [the Israelites] anger him he removes the righteous from their midst.

It follows that Israel bears a heavy burden of responsibility even for the gentiles. When Israel pleases God, the righteous among the gentiles are joined to them, and when not, not. So while gentiles as such cannot inherit the world to come, they too can enter the status of Israel, in which case they join Israel in the world to come

This the gentiles will do in exactly the way that Israel attained that status to begin with, which is by knowing God through his self-manifestation in the Torah, therefore by accepting God's rule as set forth therein. In this way the theology of the Rabbinic sages maintains its perfect consistency and inner logic: the Torah determines all things. That point is made explicit: If a gentile keeps the Torah, he is saved. But by keeping the Torah, the gentile has ceased to be gentile and become Israelite, worth even of the high priesthood. First comes the definition of how Israel becomes Israel, which is by accepting God's dominion in the Torah:

Sifra CXCIV:ii.1

1. A. "The Lord spoke to Moses saying, Speak to the Israelite people and say to them, I am the Lord your God":

B. R. Simeon b. Yohai says, "That is in line with what is said elsewhere: 'I am the Lord your God [who brought you out of the land of Egypt, out of the house of bondage]' (Ex. 20:2).

C. "'Am I the Lord, whose sovereignty you took upon yourself in Egypt?'

D. "They said to him, 'Indeed.'

E. "'Indeed you have accepted my dominion.'

F. "'They accepted my decrees: "You will have no other gods before me."'

G. "That is what is said here: 'I am the Lord your God,' meaning, 'Am I the one whose dominion you accepted at Sinai?'

H. "They said to him, 'Indeed.'

I. "'Indeed you have accepted my dominion.'

J. "'They accepted my decrees: "You shall not copy the practices of the land of Egypt where you dwelt, or of the land of Canaan to which I am taking you; nor shall you follow their laws."'"

I cite the passage to underscore how matters are defined, which is by appeal to the Torah. Then the true state of affairs emerges when the same definition explicitly is brought to bear upon the gentiles. That yields the clear inference that gentiles have the power to join themselves to Israel as fully-naturalized Israelites, so the Torah that defines their status also constitutes the ticket of admission to the world to come that Israel will enter in due course. Sages could not be more explicit than they are when they insist, the gentile ceases to be in the status of the gentile when he accepts God's rule in the Torah:

Sifra CXCIV:ii.15

15. A. "...by the pursuit of which man shall live":

B. R. Jeremiah says, "How do I know that even a gentile who keeps the Torah, lo, he is like the high priest?

C. "Scripture says, 'by the pursuit of which man shall live.'"

D. And so he says, "'And this is the Torah of the priests, Levites, and Israelites,' is not what is said here, but rather, 'This is the Torah of the man, O Lord God' (2 Sam. 7:19)."

E. And so he says, "'open the gates and let priests, Levites, and Israelites will enter it' is not what is said, but rather, 'Open the gates and let the righteous nation, who keeps faith, enter it' (Is. 26:2)."

F. And so he says, "'This is the gate of the Lord. Priests, Levites, and Israelites...' is not what is said, but rather, 'the righteous shall enter into it' (Ps. 118:20).

G. And so he says, "'What is said is not, 'Rejoice, priests, Levites, and Israelites,' but rather, 'Rejoice, O righteous, in the Lord' (Ps. 33:1)."
H. And so he says, "It is not, 'Do good, O Lord, to the priests, Levites, and Israelites,' but rather, 'Do good, O Lord, to the good, to the upright in heart' (Ps. 125:4)."
I. "Thus, even a gentile who keeps the Torah, lo, he is like the high priest."

That is not to suggest God does not rule the gentiles. He does — whether they like it or not, acknowledge him or not. God responds, also, to the acts of merit taken by gentiles, as much as to those of Israel. The upshot is, "gentile" and "Israel" classify through the presence or absence of the same traits; they form taxonomic categories that can in the case of the gentile change when that which is classified requires reclassification.

Clearly, the moral ordering of the world encompasses all humanity. But God does not neglect the gentiles or fail to exercise dominion over them. For even now, gentiles are subject to a number of commandments or religious obligations. God cares for gentiles as for Israel, he wants gentiles as much as Israel to enter the kingdom of Heaven, and he assigns to gentiles opportunities to evince their acceptance of his rule. One of these commandments is not to curse God's name, so b. San. 7:5 I.2/56a: "Any man who curses his God shall bear his sin" (Lev. 24:15)": It would have been clear had the text simply said, "A man." Why does it specify, "Any"? It serves to encompass idolaters, who are admonished not to curse the Name, just as Israelites are so admonished. Not cursing God, even while worshipping idols, seems a minimal expectation. But, in fact there are seven such religious obligations that apply to the children of Noah:

Tosefta-tractate Abodah Zarah 8:4-6

A. Concerning seven religious requirements were the children of Noah admonished:
B. setting up courts of justice, idolatry, blasphemy [cursing the Name of God], fornication, bloodshed, and thievery.

We now proceed to show how each of these religious obligations is represented as applying to gentiles as much as to Israelites:

C. Concerning setting up courts of justice— how so [how does Scripture or reason validate the claim that gentiles are to set up courts of justice]?
D. Just as Israelites are commanded to call into session in their towns courts of justice.

E. Concerning idolatry and blasphemy— how so? . . .
F. Concerning fornication— how so?
G. "On account of any form of prohibited sexual relationship on account of which an Israelite court inflicts the death-penalty, the children of Noah are subject to warning," the words of R. Meir.
H. And sages say, "There are many prohibited relationships, on account of which an Israelite court does not inflict the death-penalty and the children of Noah are [not] warned. In regard to these forbidden relationships the nations are judged in accord with the laws governing the nations.
I. "And you have only the prohibitions of sexual relations with a betrothed maiden alone."

The systemization of Scripture's evidence for the stated proposition continues:

8:5 A. For bloodshed— how so?
B. A gentile [who kills] a gentile and a gentile who kills an Israelite are liable. An Israelite [who kills] a gentile is exempt.
C. Concerning thievery?
D. [If] one has stolen, or robbed, and so too in the case of finding a beautiful captive [woman], and in similar cases:
E. a gentile in regard to a gentile, or a gentile in regard to an Israelite— it is prohibited. And an Israelite in regard to a gentile— it is permitted.
8 :6 A. Concerning a limb cut from a living beast— how so?
B. A dangling limb on a beast, [which] is not [so connected] as to bring about healing,
C. is forbidden for use by the children of Noah, and, it goes without saying, for Israelites.
D. But if there is [in the connecting flesh] sufficient [blood supply] to bring about healing,
E. it is permitted to Israelites, and, it goes without saying, to the children of Noah.

As in the case of Israelites, so the death penalty applies to a Noahide, so b. San. 7:5 I.4-5/57a: On account of violating three religious duties are children of Noah put to death: on account of adultery, murder, and blasphemy.'" R. Huna, R. Judah, and all the disciples of Rab say, "On account of seven commandments a son of Noah is put to death. The All-Merciful revealed that fact of one of them, and the same rule applies to all of them. But just as Israelites, educated in the Torah, are assumed to exhibit certain uniform virtues, e.g., forbearance, so gentiles, lacking that same education, are assumed to conform to a different model.

The gentiles thus sustain comparison and contrast with Israel, the point of ultimate division being death for the one, eternal life for the other. If Israel and the gentiles are deemed comparable, the gentiles do not acknowledge or know God, therefore, while they are like Israelites in sharing a common humanity by reason of mythic genealogy — deriving from Noah — the gentiles do not receive in a meritorious manner the blessings that God bestows upon them. God blesses the gentiles, but they do not respond properly. God gives the gentiles prophets, but the prophets to the gentiles do not measure up. So God favors the gentiles with blessings and with prophets. Not only so, but each party to humanity, Israel and the gentiles, forms its own piety as well. But with what result!

Now let us see how the gentiles are characterized in this-worldly terms, as we have noted how "being Israel" is assumed to mean a given set of virtues will mark the Israelite individual. When God blesses gentile nations, they do not acknowledge him but blaspheme, but when he blesses Israel, they glorify him and bless him; these judgments elaborate the basic principle that the gentiles do not know God, and Israel does. But what emerges here is that even when the gentiles ought to recognize God's hand in their affairs, even when God blesses them, they still deny him, turning ignorance into willfulness. What is striking is the exact balance of three gentiles as against three Israelites, all of the status of world-rulers, the common cluster, Pharaoh, Sennacherib, Nebuchadnezzar, vs. the standard cluster, David, Solomon, and Daniel:

Pesiqta deRab Kahana XXVIII:I.1

A. "On the eighth day you shall have a solemn assembly. [You shall do no laborious work, but you shall offer a burnt-offering, an offering by fire, a pleasing odor to the Lord...These you shall offer to the Lord at your appointed feasts in addition to your votive-offerings and your freewill-offerings, for your burnt-offerings and for your cereal-offerings and for your drink-offerings and for your peace-offerings]" (Numbers 29:35-9):

B. But you have increased the nation, "O Lord, you have increased the nation; [you are glorified; you have enlarged all the borders of the land]" (Is. 17:25):

The proposition having been stated, the composer proceeds to amass evidence for the two contrasting propositions, first gentile rulers:

C. You gave security to the wicked Pharaoh. Did he then call you "Lord"? Was it not with blasphemies and curses that he said, "Who is the Lord, that I should listen to his voice "(Ex. 5:2)!

D. You gave security to the wicked Sennacherib. Did he then call you "Lord"? Was it not with blasphemies and curses that he said, "Who is there among all the gods of the lands.".. (2 Kgs. 18:35).

E. You gave security to the wicked Nebuchadnezzar. Did he then call you "Lord"? Was it not with blasphemies and curses that he said, "And who is God to save you from my power" (Dan. 3:15).

Now, nicely balanced, come Israelite counterparts:

F. "...you have increased the nation; you are glorified:"

G. You gave security to David and so he blessed you: "David blessed the Lord before all the congregation "(1 Chr. 29:10).

H. You gave security to his son, Solomon, and so he blessed you: "Blessed is the Lord who has given rest to his people Israel " (1 Kgs. 8:56).

I. You gave security to Daniel and so he blessed you: "Daniel answered and said, Blessed be the name of God "(Dan. 2:20)

Here is another set of opposites — three enemies, three saints, a fair match. In each case, the Israelite responded to God's favor with blessings, and the gentile with blasphemy. In this way the gentiles show the price they pay for not knowing God but serving no-gods instead.

So now the question becomes urgent: how has this catastrophic differentiation imposed itself between Israel and the gentiles, such that the gentiles, for all their glory in the here and now, won for themselves the grave, while Israel, for all its humiliation in the present age, inherits the world to come? And the answer is self-evident from all that has been said: the gentiles reject God, whom they could and should have known in the Torah. They rejected the Torah, and all else followed. The proposition then moves in these simple steps:

[1] Israel differs from the gentiles because Israel possesses the Torah and the gentiles do not;

[2] because they do not possess the Torah, the gentiles also worship idols instead of God; and

[3] therefore God rejects the gentiles and identifies with Israel.

And where do considerations of justice and fairness enter in? Here, at a critical turning, the system reaches back into its fundamental and generative conception, that the world is ordered by justice. The Oral Torah then has to demonstrate that the same justice that governs Israel and endows Israel with the Torah dictates the fate of the gentiles and denies them the Torah. And, predictably, that demonstration must further underscore the justice of the condition of the gentiles: measure for measure must play itself out especially here.

The gentiles deprived themselves of the Torah because they rejected it, and, showing the precision of justice, they rejected the Torah because the Torah deprived them of the very practices or traits that they deemed characteristic, essential to their being. That circularity marks the tale of how things were to begin with in fact describes how things always are; it is not historical but philosophical. The gentiles' own character, the shape of their conscience, then, now, and always, accounts for their condition — which, by an act of will, as we have noted, they can change. What they did not want, that of which they were by their own word unworthy, is denied them. And what they do want condemns them. So when each nation comes under judgment for rejecting the Torah, the indictment of each is spoken out of its own mouth, its own-self-indictment then forms the core of the matter. Given what we know about the definition of Israel as those destined to live and the gentile as those not, we cannot find surprising that the entire account is set in that age to come to which the gentiles are denied entry.

When they protest the injustice of the decision that takes effect just then, they are shown the workings of the moral order, as the following quite systematic account of the governing pattern explains:

Bavli tractate Abodah Zarah 1:1 I.2/2a-b:

A. R. Hanina bar Pappa, and some say, R. Simlai, gave the following exposition [of the verse, "They that fashion a graven image are all of them vanity, and their delectable things shall not profit, and their own witnesses see not nor know" (Is. 44:9)]: "In the age to come the Holy One, blessed be He, will bring a scroll of the Torah and hold it in his bosom and say, 'Let him who has kept himself busy with it come and take his reward.' Then all the gentiles will crowd together: 'All of the nations are gathered together' (Is. 43:9). The Holy One, blessed be He, will say to them, 'Do not crowd together before me in a mob. But let each nation enter together with [2B] its scribes, 'and let the peoples be gathered together' (Is. 43:9), and the word 'people' means 'kingdom': 'and one kingdom shall be stronger than the other' (Gen. 25:23)."

We note that the players are the principal participants in world history: the Romans first and foremost, then the Persians, the other world-rulers of the age:

C. "The kingdom of Rome comes in first."

H. "The Holy One, blessed be He, will say to them, 'How have you defined your chief occupation?'

I. "They will say before him, 'Lord of the world, a vast number of marketplaces have we set up, a vast number of bathhouses we have made, a vast amount of silver and gold have we accumulated. And all of these things we have done only in behalf of Israel, so that they may define as their chief occupation the study of the Torah.'

J. "The Holy One, blessed be He, will say to them, 'You complete idiots! Whatever you have done has been for your own convenience. You have set up a vast number of marketplaces to be sure, but that was so as to set up whorehouses in them. The bathhouses were for your own pleasure. Silver and gold belong to me anyhow: "Mine is the silver and mine is the gold, says the Lord of hosts" (Hag. 2:8). Are there any among you who have been telling of "this," and "this" is only the Torah: "And this is the Torah that Moses set before the children of Israel' (Dt. 4:44)." So they will make their exit, humiliated.

The claim of Rome — to support Israel in Torah-study — is rejected on grounds that the Romans did not exhibit the right attitude, always a dynamic force in the theology. Then the other world rule enters in with its claim:

K. "When the kingdom of Rome has made its exit, the kingdom of Persia enters afterward."

M. "The Holy One, blessed be He, will say to them, 'How have you defined your chief occupation?'

N. "They will say before him, 'Lord of the world, We have thrown up a vast number of bridges, we have conquered a vast number of towns, we have made a vast number of wars, and all of them we did only for Israel, so that they may define as their chief occupation the study of the Torah.'

O. "The Holy One, blessed be He, will say to them, 'Whatever you have done has been for your own convenience. You have thrown up a vast number of bridges, to collect tolls, you have conquered a vast number of towns, to collect the corvée, and, as to making a vast number of wars, I am the one who makes wars: "The Lord is a man of war" (Ex. 19:17). Are there any among you who have been telling of "this," and "this" is only the Torah: "And this is the Torah that Moses set before the children of Israel" (Dt. 4:44).' So they will make their exit, humiliated.

R. "And so it will go with each and every nation."

As native categories, Rome and Persia are singled out, "all the other nations" play no role, for reasons with which we are already familiar. Once more the theology reaches into its deepest thought on the power of intentionality, showing that what people want is what they get.

But matters cannot be limited to the two world-empires of the present age, Rome and Iran, standing in judgment at the end of time. The theology values balance, proportion, seeks complementary relationships, and therefore treats beginnings along with endings, the one going over the ground of the other. Accordingly, a recapitulation of the same event — the gentiles' rejection of the Torah — chooses as its setting not the last judgment but the first encounter, that is, the giving of the Torah itself. In the timeless world constructed by the Oral Torah, what happens at the outset exemplifies how things always happen, and what happens at the end embodies what has always taken place. The basic thesis is identical — the gentiles cannot accept the Torah because to do so they would have to deny their very character. But the exposition retains its interest because it takes its own course.

Now the gentiles are not just Rome and Persia but others; and of special interest, the Torah is embodied in some of the ten commandments — not to murder, not to commit adultery, not to steal; then the gentiles are rejected for not keeping the seven commandments assigned to the children of Noah. The upshot is that the reason that the gentiles rejected the Torah is that the Torah prohibits deeds that the gentiles do by their very nature. The subtext here is already familiar from Chapter Three: Israel ultimately is changed by the Torah, so that Israel exhibits traits imparted by their encounter with the Torah. So too with the gentiles, by their nature they are what they are; the Torah has not changed their nature.

Once more a single standard applies to both components of humanity, but with opposite effect:

SIFRÉ TO DEUTERONOMY CCCXLIII:IV.1FF.:

1. A. Another teaching concerning the phrase, "He said, 'The Lord came from Sinai'":

B. When the Omnipresent appeared to give the Torah to Israel, it was not to Israel alone that he revealed himself but to every nation.

C. First of all he came to the children of Esau. He said to them, "Will you accept the Torah?"

D. They said to him, "What is written in it?"
E. He said to them, "'You shall not murder' (Ex. 20:13)."
F. They said to him, "The very being of 'those men' [namely, us] and of their father is to murder, for it is said, 'But the hands are the hands of Esau'"(Gen. 27:22). 'By your sword you shall live' (Gen. 27:40)."

At this point we cover new ground: other classes of gentiles that reject the Torah; now the Torah's own narrative takes over, replacing the known facts of world politics, such as the earlier account sets forth, and instead supplying evidence out of Scripture as to the character of the gentile group under discussion:

G. So he went to the children of Ammon and Moab and said to them, "Will you accept the Torah?"
H. They said to him, "What is written in it?"
I. He said to them, "'You shall not commit adultery' (Ex. 20:13)."
J. They said to him, "The very essence of fornication belongs to them [us], for it is said, 'Thus were both the daughters of Lot with child by their fathers' (Gen. 19:36)."
K. So he went to the children of Ishmael and said to them, "Will you accept the Torah?"
L. They said to him, "What is written in it?"
M. He said to them, "'You shall not steal' (Ex. 20:13)."
N. They said to him, "The very essence of their [our] father is thievery, as it is said, 'And he shall be a wild ass of a man' (Gen. 16:12)."
O. And so it went. He went to every nation, asking them, "Will you accept the Torah?"
P. For so it is said, "All the kings of the earth shall give you thanks, O Lord, for they have heard the words of your mouth" (Ps. 138:4).
Q. Might one suppose that they listened and accepted the Torah?
R. Scripture says, "And I will execute vengeance in anger and fury upon the nations, because they did not listen" (Mic. 5:14).

At this point we turn back to the obligations that God has imposed upon the gentiles; these obligations have no bearing upon the acceptance of the Torah; they form part of the ground of being, the condition of existence, of the gentiles. Yet even here, the gentiles do not accept God's authority in matters of natural law:

S. And it is not enough for them that they did not listen, but even the seven religious duties that the children of Noah indeed accepted upon themselves they could not uphold before breaking them.

T. When the Holy One, blessed be He, saw that that is how things were, he gave them to Israel.

What then does God hope to accomplish through exercising dominion over Israel by means of the nations? It is the medium for reestablishing his rule over humanity, embodied in Israel, through Israel's own intentionality. Israel is Adam's counterpart, only empowered by the Torah to bend its will to God's will. How does this take place? First of all, Israel will be lead through suffering in exile to repentance, at which point God will forgive them. That point sages learn at Leviticus Chapter Twenty-Six, as most of what they have to say they derive from Scripture in accord with their governing hermeneutics, which, they would claim, they have to begin with derived from Scripture:

SIFRA CCLXIX:II.1, 3

A. "But if they confess their iniquity and the iniquity of their fathers [in their treachery which they committed against me, and also in walking contrary to me, so that I walked contrary to them and brought them into the land of their enemies; if then their uncircumcised heart is humbled and they make amends for their iniquity; then I will remember my covenant with Jacob, and I will remember my covenant also with Isaac and my covenant also with Abraham, and I will remember the land. But the land shall be left by them and enjoy its Sabbaths while it lies desolate without them; and they shall make amends for their iniquity, because they spurned my ordinances, and their soul abhorred my statutes. Yet for all that, when they are in the land of their enemies, I will not spurn them, neither will I abhor them so as to destroy them utterly and break my covenant with them; for I am the Lord their God; but I will for their sake remember the covenant with their forefathers whom I brought forth out of the land of Egypt in the sight of the nations, that I might be their God: I am the Lord. These are the statutes and ordinances and laws which the Lord made between him and the people of Israel on Mount Sinai by Moses]" (Lev. 26:40-46):

B. This is how things are as to repentance,

C. for as soon as they confess their sins, I forthwith revert and have mercy on them,

D. as it is said, "But if they confess their iniquity and the iniquity of their fathers in their treachery which they committed against me."

The second point is that God will never permit Israel to remove itself from his dominion; willy-nilly they will remain his kingdom:

3. A. "...and brought them into the land of their enemies":
B. This is a good deal for Israel.
C. For the Israelites are not to say, "Since we have gone into exile among the gentiles, let us act like them."
D. [God speaks:] "I shall not let them, but I shall call forth prophets against them, who will bring them back to the right way under my wings."
E. And how do we know?
F. "What is in your mind shall never happen, the thought, 'Let us be like the nations, like the tribes of the countries, and worship wood and stone.' 'As I live,' says the Lord God, 'surely with a might hand and an outstretched arm and with wrath poured out, I will be king over you. [I will bring you out from the peoples and gather you out of the countries where you are scattered, with a mighty hand and an outstretched arm and with wrath poured out'" (Ez. 20:33-3).
G. Whether you like it or not, with or without your consent, I shall establish my dominion over you."

Israel subject to the gentiles then gains the opportunity to repent and reconcile itself with God, and that is the plan that God has devised to overcome the workings of strict justice; exile and subjugation then form acts of mercy on God's part, just as Abraham had foreseen when he wisely chose the rule of the nations over Gehenna.

The final question that requires attention returns us to our starting point, the comparison of Israel and the nations, in the present case, the Israelite with the gentile. That is framed in terms of Israel and Adam, meaning, the sector of humanity within, and the part of humanity outside of, the circle of the Torah. By reason of disobedience Adam sinned and was justly punished by exile from Eden; that represented an act of mercy, he was not wiped out, as Eve had said he and she would be. Because of disobedience Israel sinned and was justly punished by exile from the Land of Israel, counterpart to Eden. But then is Israel not just another Adam — rebellious and permanently punished on that account? There is a distinction, one that makes all the difference. The Torah, carrying with it the possibility of repentance, changes Israel's condition.

Israel is like Adam, but Israel is the Other, the Last Adam, the opposite of Adam. We shall now systematically compare Adam and Israel, the first man and the last, and show how the story of Adam matches the story of Israel — but with a difference:

Genesis Rabbah XIX:IX.1-2

2. A. R. Abbahu in the name of R. Yosé bar Haninah: "It is written, 'But they are like a man [Adam], they have transgressed the covenant' (Hos. 6:7).
   B. "'They are like a man,' specifically, like the first man. [We shall now compare the story of the first man in Eden with the story of Israel in its land.]

Now the composer identifies an action in regard to Adam with a counterpart Action in regard to Israel, in each case matching verse for verse, beginning with Eden and Adam:

C. "'In the case of the first man, I brought him into the garden of Eden, I commanded him, he violated my commandment, I judged him to be sent away and driven out, but I mourned for him, saying "How..."'[which begins the book of Lamentations, hence stands for a lament, but which, as we just saw, also is written with the consonants that also yield, 'Where are you'].
D. "'I brought him into the garden of Eden,' as it is written, 'And the Lord God took the man and put him into the garden of Eden' (Gen. 2:15).
E. "'I commanded him,' as it is written, 'And the Lord God commanded...' (Gen. 2:16).
F. "'And he violated my commandment,' as it is written, 'Did you eat from the tree concerning which I commanded you' (Gen. 3:11).
G. "'I judged him to be sent away,' as it is written, ''And the Lord God sent him from the garden of Eden' (Gen. 3:23).
H. "'And I judged him to be driven out.' 'And he drove out the man' (Gen. 3:24).
I. "'But I mourned for him, saying, "How..".' 'And he said to him, "Where are you"' (Gen. 3:9), and the word for 'where are you' is written, 'How...'

Now comes the systematic comparison of Adam and Eden with Israel and the Land of Israel:

> J. "'So too in the case of his descendants, [God continues to speak,] I brought them into the Land of Israel, I commanded them, they violated my commandment, I judged them to be sent out and driven away but I mourned for them, saying, "How..."'
>
> K. "'I brought them into the Land of Israel.' 'And I brought you into the land of Carmel' (Jer. 2:7).
>
> L. "'I commanded them.' 'And you, command the children of Israel' (Ex. 27:20). 'Command the children of Israel' (Lev. 24:2).
>
> M. "'They violated my commandment.' 'And all Israel have violated your Torah' (Dan. 9:11).
>
> N. "'I judged them to be sent out.' 'Send them away, out of my sight and let them go forth' (Jer 15:1).
>
> O. "'...and driven away.' 'From my house I shall drive them' (Hos. 9:15).
>
> P. "'But I mourned for them, saying, "How..."' 'How has the city sat solitary, that was full of people' (Lam. 1:1)."

Here we end where we began, Israel in exile from the Land, like Adam in exile from Eden. But the Torah is clear that there is a difference, which we shall address in its proper place: Israel can repent.

So to conclude: the just world order is comprised by the division of humanity into Israel with the Torah, and the gentiles with their idols. The one is destined to life eternal with God, the other to the grave, there to spend eternity. World order then finds its center and focus in Israel, and whatever happens that counts under Heaven's gaze takes place in relationship to Israel. That division yields rich and dense details but only a simple story, easily retold. In a purposeful act of benevolence, the just God created the world in so orderly a way that the principle of justice and equity governs throughout. Fair rules apply equally to all persons and govern all circumstances. God not only created man but made himself known to man through the Torah. But man, possessed of free will, enjoys the choice of accepting and obeying the Torah, therefore living in the kingdom of Heaven, or rejecting the Torah and God in favor of idolatry and idols.

Now we realize the full potentiality contained in the simple doctrines with which we began: that those who accept the Torah are called Israel, and the others are called gentiles. The gentiles hate Israel because of the Torah, and they also hate God. But the world as now constituted is such that the gentiles rule, and Israel is subjugated. Where is the justice in that inversion of right, with God's people handed over to the charge of God's enemies? Israel has sinned, so rebelled against God, and the gentiles then form God's instrument for the punishment of Israel. God's justice governs, the world conforms to orderly rules, embedded in the very structure of creation. Israel's own condition stands as the surest testimony of the world's good and just order. That guarantee is for now and all time to come.

IV

When Paul thinks of "Israel," he thinks about salvation, a position the sages' system maintained as well. That is why Paul treats the word "sinner" and the word "gentile" as synonymous: "Jews, not gentile sinners." And in that context, he frames the issue: Christ versus Torah ("works of the law"). If the one has solved the problem of the human condition and character, the solution of the other is not needed. But then Paul's argument is not with Peter, because to him, Peter's position is in the exact sense of the word, irrelevant. With Peter there can be no argument about salvation, only a political modus vivendi, which, Galatians indicates, has broken down.

Now Paul's stress on salvation not through the Torah but through Christ proves emblematic of his entire system and a counterpart to the congruent system of the Rabbinic sages. He concurs with the logic embodied, also, in the sages' Judaic system: the issue is the redemption of humanity from the human condition embodied by Adam and Eve. For the sages the narrative of the Hebrew Scriptures leads to the focus on Israel as Adam's counterpart, the Torah as the medium of regeneration (and consequent justification, I think we must agree to add). That is why for both Paul and sages the definition of who and what is Israel is critical; from that all else follows. No wonder, then, that, within his system's logic, Paul immediately focuses upon the figure of Abraham and identifies exactly the issue of systemic concern: "Abraham 'believed God and it was reckoned to him as righteousness'" (Gal. 3:6/Gen. 15:6).

Since these remarks strike me as typical of an outsider to a field — self-evident and not surprising — let me justify making them by reference to a single, a current reading of the same passages of Galatians, one that has attracted a fair amount of attention, and even a prize from the National Jewish Book Council (as though Jewish book councils possessed the learning to give prizes in the New Testament field!).

I refer to Mark D. Nanos, who, in a remarkable misconstruction of the Judaism presented by the Mishnah, Talmuds, and Midrash, takes the view:

> Paul turned to the gentiles with the gospel so that the 'stumbling' of Israel might reconsider the arrival of the promised times and the message of good news for themselves and for the world. We also found that when Paul argued for gentile inclusion in Christ without becoming Jews that he did not appeal to the nullifying of the Torah

> because of the supersession of Christ. He appealed, instead to the inherent truth of monotheism and developed his position within the context of the *Shema*: "Or is God the God of Jews only? Is he not the God of gentiles also?" "Of course, for he is the one God of all" was Paul's uncompromising reply. The Paul of Romans believed that faith in Christ 'established' Torah; it certainly did not make it obsolete.[3]

As a consumer, not a producer, in this field, I must say, I find this claim counter-intuitive, and also contrary to two millennia of exegesis. But that impressionistic judgment carries, and should carry, no weight.

Where my judgment may carry weight, it concerns the reading of the Judaic-systemic position before us: the system that equates "Judaism" with what we learn in the Rabbinic documents about the recitation of the *Shema*, about monotheism. From the perspective of the Rabbinic sages as I understand them, this statement of Nanos is incomprehensible. If gentiles accept monotheism as embodied in the *Shema*, they become Israel. That is what is involved in reciting the *Shema*, as everyone knows: accepting God's unity and dominion is what the Israelite does morning and night in proclaiming that formula. And one who accepts God's unity and dominion is "Israel" — that is what "Israel" means. Where Nanos formulates matters in a category I do not think sages can have grasped (in the present context) is the use of "God of Jews/God of gentiles." That is not the appropriate category and violates the rules of category-formation. He needs to say "God of Israel," and then its opposite is, "the no-God of the gentile." Then the rest follows. Then Nanos's stress on Paul's "Monotheistic insistence that to do so [practice circumcision[] would be to compromise God's oneness, for the One God of Israel was the one God of non-Israel too," is systemically incomprehensible. To accept the One God is *to be*, to constitute, Israel. "The circumcised" refers to "Israel," even those Israelites who are not circumcised, so the Mishnah maintains:

> G. [If he said,] "Qonam if I derive benefit from the uncircumcised," he is permitted [to derive benefit] from uncircumcised Israelites but prohibited [from deriving benefit] from circumcised gentiles.
>
> H. "Qonam if I derive benefit from the circumcised" — he is prohibited [to derive benefit] from uncircumcised Israelites and permitted [to derive benefit] from circumcised gentiles.
>
> I. For the word "uncircumcised" is used only as a name for gentiles, as it is written, "For all the nations are uncircumcised, and the whole house of Israel is uncircumcised at heart" (Jer. 9:26).
>
> J. And it says, "This uncircumcised Philistine (1 Sam. 17:36).

[3] *The Mystery of Romans. The Jewish Context of Paul's Letter* (Minneapolis, 1996: Fortress).

K. And it says, Lest the daughters of the Philistines rejoice, lest the daughters of the uncircumcised triumph (1 Sam. 1:20).

M. Nedarim 3:11

So the focus on circumcision treats the metaphor for Israel as the very definition of that which is metaphorized! The emphasis on circumcision as monothetic taxon of "Israel" derives from the logic of Paul's system, Abraham having found God before, and without the condition of, circumcision. To say that sages will not have understood Paul in Nanos's reading of him is no criticism of Nanos's reading of Paul. It is only to call into question the systemic logic that Nanos follows in his reading of Paul. If, as I maintain, the systemic issue is the antonyms, Israel/gentiles, and if gentiles by definition are idolaters, then sages' view follows. To understand Paul's position, we should have to have a much clearer picture of what he means by the Israel/gentile antonym than he gives us in the passage at hand. If a gentile is a monotheist and worships the God made known in Israel's Scripture, then he is an Israelite. And if not, then he is not a monotheist and does not know God. Who, then, can Nanos's non-Israelite monotheists be? They are none other than that Israel after the spirit of Romans, about whom Paul has thought so deeply. In that case, the received reading of Romans turns out to have much to recommend it.

V

What does systemic analysis, the inquiry into the coherence, balance, proportion, and order, of a religious account of the social order that concerns way of life, world view, and a theory of the social entity that realizes the one and explains matters through the other, contribute? In the present context, that approach, seeing a man's thought whole and in perspective, in Paul's, Peter's, and James's cases, in the model of a Judaism, a religious theory of the social order that privileges ancient Israelite Scripture, serves. Specifically, it allows us to understand the way the parts hold together, making a statement that transcends their sum. In simple terms, I mean to offer an explanation, out of the resources of a system kindred to his, of Paul's discourse with James and Peter in Galatians 2. In a word, Paul scarcely engages with James's system, and he treats Peter as a political problem, a charlatan, not a worthy contender over truth. James will not eat with gentiles. Peter will except when he won't. Paul evinces slight respect for either position, because (in my theory of matters) neither pertains. But Peter's is beyond all comprehension.

May I offer a modest proposal to explain matters. If the issue is salvific, then, as Paul frames matters, it also is eschatological in a perfectly personal sense: it is Christ who lives in Paul, who has died and come back to life: "It is not I who live but Christ who lives in me, and the life I now live in the flesh I live by faith in the son of God." If we take as a given that the resurrection of the dead and the judgment take place at the end of days, then we do not claim too much if we allege, for Paul the issue is not salvation in general terms — as the sages frame matters — but salvation at the critical moment in the story of humanity from Adam to Adam. For the very reason that Adam provides a systemic key, the realized eschatological moment provides a systemic key: it is the same lock, opened by the same key. Here the sages' system and Paul's clearly part company, for the sages, start to finish, look forward to the eschaton in future time, to be signaled by a Messiah, and for now, they find a place for sanctification, a critical task to be accomplished thereby.

The contrast between Paul's and the sages' reading of the salvific story — a difference in detail of which each system can make sense — yields a typology that may illuminate matters. The issue of Peter, James, and Paul in Galatians may be seen to turn on three readings of the *kairos*, the meaning of the moment, James's, Peter's, and Paul's. Within this theory, the end-time — resurrection, judgment, eternal life — has not taken place, and a Christology of an other-than-eschatological Christ must be aborning. Or the end-time — death, resurrection, judgment, eternal life — has taken place, and a Christology of a realized eschaton follows. Or, in the middle, the end-time of which the prophets spoke as "the end of days" has commenced but not come to fulfillment: an interstitial age has taken place.

The three positions are embodied, obviously, by James, Paul, and Peter. For James, the Torah remains man's medium of regeneration, sanctification his task, and Jesus the harbinger of what is to be. But James, by this theory, cannot speak of the end of days at all; it cannot be an issue within his logic. For Paul, the Torah no longer pertains, whether as to purity at table or even as to circumcision, for to be "Israel" is signaled not by circumcision, which is post facto as Abraham shows, but by Christ, through whom man is reborn (as Paul says in so many words right in the present context). That means, man has died and been raised from the dead, judged, and accorded eternal life. It is Peter's position that mediates. Within the present theory, Peter's theory of the kairos — Christ has come, but the hour has not yet reached fulfillment — will shape a position on the salvific promise of the works of the law of the Torah between James's and Paul's. For Peter, as for the rabbis, sanctification forms a preparation for salvation, a condition, a means to an end — but only that.

James's and Paul's positions prove to be simply incompatible. Paul cannot accuse James of hypocrisy, because he finds his position unbelievable to begin with: systemically beyond all logic or comprehension, irrational. But while Paul can never agree with Peter, Peter can agree with Paul: eat with gentiles. The problem is, Paul cannot agree with Peter for reasons common to the system of each: an issue that can be joined, one with the other. And that is the crux of matters, lies in the exact meaning of the word "crux." In a simple phrase, Peter (within my proposed typology) should say: "Yet but not yet: begun, not realized and so not ended." To take a simple metaphor: the sun has risen, but it is not high noon. Then he can in full consistency agree that circumcision still serves but eat with gentiles: "yet, but not yet." Within this theory of matters Peter's Christology should find in Christ the realization and fulfillment of the promises of the Torah about Adam's regeneration: he should be the last Adam. But while Paul has died and risen from the grave in the full realization of the resurrection and judgment — that is why he can speak so certainly of justification, meaning in Rabbinic language, "standing in judgment" — Peter has not. On what has commenced Paul and Peter then can and do concur (within this theory). They differ only on where matters now stand in the eschatological crisis.

With James Paul cannot argue, with Peter out of stupefaction he cannot even engage. Paul's and Peter's orbits do not quite intersect; they bring the other into range: hence the stupefaction. Accordingly, Paul dismisses as hypocritical, which is to say, willful and merely political, what is in fact a component of a perfectly rational system — a system whose rationality intersects with that of Paul. The positions of Paul and Peter are concentric, but not totally so; where they differ is on what from a distance appears minor, but what is systemically critical for Paul and contingent for Peter, the question of when: how long, O Lord? For Peter what is in yet a little while for Paul is fully present, at this hour. Hence the frustration of Paul at Peter's equanimity. And what of James? Peter can appear to accord with James's view of the task of the time, which is, sanctification, even while in fact sharing Paul's confidence in the salvific reading of matters. The upshot is, he takes a mediating position, but that is a happenstance, an effect of what animates his system, which is his own rationality: a judgment as to where we now stand. At least, so matters appear to an outsider to the subject.